Criminal Justice
Recent Scholarship

Edited by
Marilyn McShane and Frank P. Williams III

A Series from LFB Scholarly

The Family Context of Childhood Delinquency

Justin W. Patchin

LFB Scholarly Publishing LLC
New York 2006

Library of Congress Cataloging-in-Publication Data

Patchin, Justin W., 1977-
  The family context of childhood delinquency / Justin W. Patchin.
      p. cm. -- (Criminal justice recent scholarship)
  Includes bibliographical references and index.
  ISBN 1-59332-154-6 (alk. paper)
  1. Juvenile delinquents--United States--Family relationships. 2.
Juvenile delinquents--Rehabilitation--United States. 3. Social work
with juvenile delinquents--United States. 4. Community-based
corrections--United States. I. Title.
  HV9104.P38 2006
  364.36--dc22

                              2006019393

ISBN 1-59332-154-6

Printed on acid-free 250-year-life paper.

Manufactured in the United States of America.

To Jill, for standing by me through it all.

Table of Contents

List of Tables

ix

List of Figures

xi

Acknowledgments

I greatly appreciate the guidance and support I have received from Tim Bynum, Christina DeJong-Schwitzer, Cynthia Perez McCluskey, and Bill Davidson. Your hands have helped to shape this work beyond what I had envisioned. I would also like to thank Randall Beger, Amanda Burgess-Proctor, Sameer Hinduja, Beth Huebner, and Joe Schafer for reviewing previous drafts of this manuscript. Despite their best efforts, they cannot be held responsible for my failure to follow their prudent guidance. I want to extend a special thanks to my wife Jill and my parents Mike and Kathie for always being by my side. My sisters Jennifer and Theresa have also given me particular insight into adolescent development from my perspective as a middle child. The love and encouragement of my family has sustained me at difficult professional and personal times and testifies to the importance of this work. Finally, I want to thank God for being in my life everyday. But for His grace, I may have been the subject rather than the author of this work.

CHAPTER 1
Introduction

For decades social scientists have attempted to identify and understand the etiology of juvenile crime and to determine factors that contribute to the persistence or desistance of antisocial behaviors. A better understanding of such factors would allow policymakers and practitioners to develop and implement effective interventions to ameliorate the antecedent conditions of aggressive and delinquent behavior. One such factor that has been identified as playing a pivotal role in the development or cessation of deviant tendencies is the relationship between child and parent.

Concomitant with this interest in the relationship between family functioning and crime in recent years has been a concern that interventions aimed at rehabilitating delinquent youth have largely failed (Gottfredson & Hirschi, 1990; Whitehead & Lab, 1989). Particularly obstinate are serious and violent offenders who seem impervious to any effort at intervention.

To be sure, most adolescents engage in behaviors that could be defined as deviant or even delinquent. Much of these activities involve rebelling at their youthful status by engaging in adult-like behaviors such as smoking, drinking, or minor theft. While ubiquitous and relatively age appropriate among middle and late adolescents, children who engage in these same behaviors at an early age (prior to age 13 or so) are at an elevated risk to engage in a variety of antisocial behaviors throughout their life course (Burns et al., 2003; Elliott, Huizinga, & Ageton, 1985; Loeber, 1982; Moffitt, 1993; Tolan & Gorman-Smith, 1998). Moreover, children who engage in *serious* delinquent activities (e.g., serious assault, home invasion, robbery, sexual assault) are among the most at risk for a lifetime of criminal behavior (Loeber, Farrington, & Waschbusch, 1998; Loeber & Farrington, 2001). As such, it is important to identify not only the causes of early childhood delinquent behaviors, but also effective intervention strategies to interrupt this potentially problematic developmental trajectory.

This book represents an up-to-date and succinct review of the empirical and theoretical literature regarding the association between family relationships (e.g., discipline, supervision, emotional affect) and delinquency. It also moves beyond the research that is cited by exploring more fully these dynamics among serious childhood offenders. While volumes have been written about the adverse outcomes linked to dysfunctional familial relationships and problematic parenting practices, much less is known about how these issues apply to young children who engage in serious and violent behaviors and more importantly how we can use these lessons to develop effective interventions to address the antisocial behaviors among this group.

In general, this book will attempt to further investigate the ways in which family relationships can provide a supportive environment to serious childhood offenders within an intervention context. Because all serious childhood offenders will at some point end up in an intervention, it is also important to examine the characteristics of successful interventions that target this population. It is argued that the family domain must be considered in any comprehensive intervention aimed at delinquent youth, particularly childhood offenders.

As such, it is hypothesized that individuals who report having "strong" relationships with their parents are likely to fare better in intervention programs than those who do not.

Characteristics of strong familial relationships include: regular communication, respect, trust, and general positive emotional affect. It is hypothesized that youth who begin an intervention experience already having a strong relationship with their parent(s) may not require family-based programming to the extent that others do. A related hypothesis examines the extent to which youth who receive family-based programming or otherwise improve their relationship with their parent(s) during an intervention are more likely to desist offending. Specifically, this study analyzed whether serious young offenders who were involved in a comprehensive, community-based intervention were differentially successful at abstaining from offending based on specific family characteristics (family bond and structure) and whether or not they received family-based programming while involved in the intervention.

In determining the importance of family relationships on delinquency desistance, this study will proceed in several stages. First, this chapter will provide a broad overview of the extant research on families and delinquency, and review what is known about serious, violent, and early juvenile offenders, the sample of concern in the current analysis. Chapter Two will discuss the theoretical foundations of a relationship between family functioning and delinquency. Focusing primarily on control-based theories, several popular perspectives will be examined insofar as they incorporate familial relations as a primary component in their explanatory models. Next, Chapter Three will discuss the current sample and methods employed to test the relationship between family relations and delinquency among childhood offenders. Chapter Four will present results of statistical tests performed to assess the importance of family relationships in juvenile programming. Logistic regression and Hierarchical Linear Modeling will be employed in this regard. Finally, Chapter Five will discuss the strengths and limitations of the current study, highlight areas for future research, and point to specific theoretical and policy implications to be drawn from its results.

FAMILY RELATIONS AND DELINQUENCY

In all cultures, historical and modern, the family has been, and continues to be, the central socializing institution responsible for instilling in youth a set of norms, values, beliefs, and ideals (Loury, 1987). The failure of families to accomplish this task can result in negative consequences for the individual and society at large. During the 1950's, several researchers examined the role of families in delinquency causation. While largely unpopular at the time (Laub & Sampson, 1991; Sampson & Laub, 1993), Sheldon and Eleanor Glueck (1950; 1952; 1962) provided much of the impetus for focusing on family relationships and delinquency causation. Others at that time were also involved in research attempting to disentangle the association between family relationships and crime (Nye, 1958; Reiss, 1951). Recently, however, there has been increased attention directed toward the role parents play in delinquency prevention (Anderson, 2002; Bank & Burraston, 2001; Cernkovick & Giordano, 1987; Gerard & Buehler, 1999; Gorman-Smith, Tolan, Zelli, & Huesmann, 1996; Gorman-Smith, Tolan, Loeber, & Henry, 1998; Heck & Walsh, 2000; McCord, 1991; Thornberry et al., 1999; Unnever, Cullen, & Agnew, 2006; Wright, Cullen, & Miller, 2001).

This section will review the family and delinquency literature for the purpose of better understanding the association between family relationships and juvenile delinquency. Explored are several ways in which a negative family environment can be a risk factor for children to engage in delinquent activities and ways that effective parenting can act as a buffer to insulate at-risk youth from participating in deviance.

Dynamics within the family can influence whether a youth will engage in anti-normative activities. To be sure, most researchers agree that "bad" parenting is a compelling cause of delinquent behavior (Unnever et al., 2006). For example, children of parents who are constantly quarrelling or are otherwise incompatible with each other are more likely to develop negative traits such as extreme restlessness and destructiveness–both common antecedents to delinquency (Glueck & Glueck, 1962). Also, lack of emotional ties between parents or between parent and child contribute to involvement in maladaptive behavior (Hirschi, 1969; Glueck & Glueck, 1962). Needle, Su, Doherty, Lavee, and Brown (1988), for example, identified family instability, deficient family cohesion, and lack of quality relationships between parents and children as predictors of adolescent substance use. Loeber and Stouthamer-Loeber (1986) identified four paradigms that outline how the family can negatively influence adolescent behavior. These areas include: neglect, conflict, deviant behaviors and attitudes, and disruption. The following sub-section will discuss each of these paradigms in turn.

The Neglect Paradigm

Parents who fail to enforce their demands and lack control over the individual child both inside and outside the home may foster delinquent tendencies (Nye, 1958). Neglectful parents either explicitly ignore the behaviors in which their children are engaging, or are unprepared to effectively address the behavior. Specifically, parents who are afraid to cause tension in the family often allow their children too much latitude in conduct. Instead of punishing children for breaking curfew, for example, neglectful parents regularly look past these seemingly trivial violations. Overly permissive parents are usually indulgent to their children and give in to their every desire. These parents fail to set limits to provide proper structure and regulate boundaries within which their children should behave (Cobb, 2001). As such, permissive parents are loved by their children because few constraints are placed on the child. There are, of course, negative ramifications stemming from this parental indifference. Due to this lack style of parenting, children of permissive parents often have trouble developing friendships and lack the ability to regulate their emotions (Cobb, 2001). These issues can manifest themselves in frequent quarrels at school or involvement in other delinquent behavior (i.e., shoplifting) as the youth attempts to gain friends.

Two common forms of neglect are lack of supervision and lack of involvement. A large body of literature demonstrates the deleterious effects of improper parental supervision (Glueck & Glueck, 1950; Hirschi, 1969; Patterson, 1980). Effective parents are aware of their children's activities, the friends they associate with, and the places they hang out (Cobb, 2001). Parents who do not adequately supervise their children will be unable to effectively control their behavior through positive reinforcement and appropriate punishment. In their meta-analysis of longitudinal studies, Loeber and Stouthamer-Loeber (1986:29) found that parental supervision was "…among the most powerful predictors of juvenile conduct problems and delinquency." In the Richmond Youth Project, Hirschi (1969) found that youth who reported that their parents knew where they were and who they associated with were less likely to engage in delinquent activities. It has also been suggested that inadequate or neglectful supervision contributes to association with deviant peers (Ingram, Patchin, Huebner, McCluskey, and Bynum, 2006; Warr, 2002, 2005).

In addition, attachment to one's parents can result in decreased delinquency through a process known as "virtual supervision" (Hirschi, 1969). Virtual or indirect supervision occurs when children who are strongly attached to their parent(s) consider the response of their parents when participating in certain activities, even if a parent is not immediately supervising them. Fearing a negative response from a parent who may learn of proscribed activities, youth will often refrain from engaging in forbidden activities.

Parental involvement is also an important protective factor. On the other hand, parents who are not actively involved in activities with their children may be increasing their risk for delinquency. Of the twenty-nine studies reviewed by Loeber and Stouthamer-Loeber (1986), twenty-two reported a significant association between lack of parental involvement and delinquency. Moreover, this relationship remained whether considering self-reported or official delinquency and a number of different outcome measures (e.g., frequency and variety of offenses).

The Conflict Paradigm

Within the conflict paradigm, parents demonstrate overly harsh disciplinary approaches ranging from emotional abuse to extreme physical assault. As a result of inconsistent or harsh disciplining, children often rebel and escalate disruptive behavior. A reciprocal relationship ensues whereby both parent and child view each other as adversaries. Frustrated adolescents may look toward their peer networks or other sources for support in environments where parents are abusive. These relationships, then, lead to higher rates of delinquency, substance abuse, and the development of inappropriate sexual identities (Bank & Burraston, 2001; Hill, Howell, Hawkins, & Battin-Pearson, 1999; Rebellon & Van Grundy, 2005; Wallace & Bachman, 1991; Warr, 2002, 2005).

An abusive home environment can be characterized in many different ways. Youth can be physically, sexually, or emotionally abused and/or neglected. Even if not physically injured, there is consensus that maltreatment can result in lasting emotional and cognitive damage (Hunner & Walker, 1981; Kaplan, Pelcovitz, & Labruna, 1999). In a comprehensive review of literature examining the link between child maltreatment and delinquency, Knutson (1995) concluded that youth who are seriously maltreated are at risk to becoming antisocial adolescents and aggressive adults (see also Besharov, 1987; McCord, 1989). Interestingly, Ireland, Smith, and Thornberry (2002) found that maltreatment in *childhood only* was not significantly related to delinquency and drug use in late adolescence, however *adolescent or persistent maltreatment* (occurring during both childhood and adolescence) was significantly related to these negative outcomes. This finding stresses the importance of research from a developmental perspective which identifies the timing and duration of life events as important considerations.

A wealth of empirical information exists indicating that abusive discipline practices are related to a "lack of parenting skills, social and economic disadvantage, and parental psychopathology and substance abuse" (Bank & Burraston, 2001:196). In this way, an abusive environment often represents a constellation of negative stimuli that can affect youth. Moreover, inconsistent discipline may indirectly affect the long-term development of youth by increasing the likelihood of maltreatment, neglect, and sibling conflict (Bank & Burraston, 2001; Patterson, 1980). High rates of sibling conflict, for instance, has been identified as being significantly associated (r=.80) with antisocial activities in adolescence and criminality in adulthood (Bank & Burraston, 2001). Sibling antisocial behavior was also predictive of adolescent gang membership (Hill et al., 1999).

As these studies indicate, parents who harshly punish their children may put them at a greater risk for future delinquency (Miller & Knutson, 1997). Additionally, some parents may punish severely at one time but ignore the same behavior at another. This disciplining style can actually teach a difficult child to become more oppositional as undesirable behaviors are inconsistently punished (Wahler, 1987). Children become unclear as to what behavior is acceptable and what is not. A proper balance, then, must involve appropriate levels of discipline whereby the youth understands the purpose behind such response (Patterson, 1980).

The myriad number of negative consequences associated with child abuse are important and well documented, and, as such, the topic warrants more consideration than is available here (for reviews, see Jonson, 1998; Knutson, 1995; Rebellon & Van Gundy, 2005; Salmelainen, 1996; Veltman & Browne, 2001). As Bank and Burraston (2001:211) note, "when we maltreat our kids, they are more likely to get hurt, to get into trouble with the law, and to harm others."

The Deviant Behavior and Attitudes Paradigm

Parents who are themselves deviant may implicitly or explicitly pass these behaviors on to their progeny. For example, while the causal process is not completely understood, research indicates that delinquents are more likely than nondelinquents to have been raised by criminal fathers (Glueck & Glueck, 1962; Hirschi, 1969). It is unclear whether childhood deviance is learned from parents who are involved in antisocial activities (Bandura, 1986; Burgess & Akers, 1966; Skinner, 1953); if there is something about the environment from within which parents and children are raised (Brooks-Gunn, Duncan, Klebanov, & Sealand, 1993); or if there is some biological component to crime (Wilson & Herrnstein, 1985). Indeed, it is likely a combination of these factors affect the developmental outcomes of children. Whatever the cause, criminological consensus concludes that parental deviance[1] is a strong correlate of adolescent offending.

When one or both parents are involved in criminal behaviors or substance abuse, similar propensities may be fostered among their children. Sampson and Laub (1993) also found evidence that parental deviance pushes children towards deviant peers. Similarly, youth who are reared by alcoholic fathers are more likely to develop criminogenic traits such as hostility and unconventionality and, correspondingly, are at a greater risk for delinquency (Glueck & Glueck, 1962). Pathology among mothers also plays an important role in the development of deviant predilections. Indeed, histories of criminal involvement

---

[1] It is important to note that in the current text "deviance" (or "deviant behavior") is not used interchangeably with other, more specific terms, such as offending, delinquency, or crime. Instead, it is used to suggest a broader form of maladaptive behavior that may or may not be regulated by law.

and alcoholism of the mother was found to be more prevalent in delinquent youth when compared to nondelinquent youth (Glueck & Glueck, 1962). In fact, the negative effects of a pathologic mother appeared more influential in predicting delinquency than pathology of the father (Glueck & Glueck, 1962). It has also been found that younger children are more susceptible to the pathology of their mothers while older children are often more affected by the behavior of their fathers (Connell & Goodman, 2002).

Growing up with parents who are openly involved in deviant activities can also have detrimental effects for youth as they develop their own identity. A major step in the development of an adolescent's identity involves the differentiation of self from the ego mass of family (Bowen, 1978). Familial conflict associated with parental involvement in deviant activities can have at least two negative consequences for youth: (1) the child may learn about deviant activities from his or her parents or at least perceive that they are normal behaviors; or, (2) if a child recognizes that the behavior is counter to what he or she has learned elsewhere (schools or friends) he or she may detach from the familial unit too early. Either trajectory can lead to other potentially problematic outcomes. For example, one negative manifestation involves retreating to the acceptance of a deviant gang. Indeed, Hill and colleagues (1999:302) found that gang members reported "frequent conflict and abuse among their parents, child abuse, family member alcoholism and drug addiction, and family trouble with the police."

The relationship between parental deviance and the antisocial behavior of children may suggest a biologically determined component to crime causation (Wilson & Herrnstein, 1985). That is, some genetic predisposition towards criminality is passed from parent to child. To be sure, there are considerable volumes of research suggestive of a relationship between biology and crime (Mednick & Christainsen, 1977; Wilson & Herrnstein, 1985). Sampson and Laub (1993) argued, instead, that deviant parents put their children at risk for delinquency not because of some genetic trait, but because their parenting is compromised due to their own illicit activities. For example, inebriated parents cannot effectively supervise their children and may punish inconsistently or harshly. Indeed, Sampson and Laub's (1993) analyses supported the assertion that parental deviance negatively affects their discipline and supervision abilities (see also Patterson, 1980). Further, Sampson and Laub (1993:69) argued that "(p)arenting is perhaps the most demanding of conventional roles, and we expect that deviance in the adult world will manifest itself in disrupted styles of child socialization." Conversely, strong parenting skills can buffer youth with at-risk traits, such as irritability or poor temperament, from engaging in antisocial activities. As such, the biological argument may be largely irrelevant once proper parenting is considered (Sampson & Laub, 1993).

Gottfredson & Hirschi (1990) offer a different interpretation of the relationship between parental deviance and childhood delinquency. These theorists suggest that adults who are deviant are also poor at child rearing. Both of these behaviors are manifestations of the same latent trait: low self-control. Adults with low self-control, therefore, often have children who have been improperly trained, and as a result, have low self-control themselves. Similarly, Moffitt (1993:681) suggests that "...parents of children who are difficult to manage often lack the necessary psychological and physical resources to cope constructively with a difficult child." Patterson (1982:11) concurred, noting that "(p)arents of aggressive children are generally unskilled, but they are particularly unskilled in their use of punishment for deviant behavior." This argument is also similar to Sampson and Laub's (1993) claim that deviant adults simply lack effective parenting skills.

Because there are few children who grow up away from their deviant parents, it is often difficult to distinguish between the role of environment and biology in producing delinquent children (Loeber, 1987). Despite these limitations, Rowe and Osgood (1984:535) noted that "(t)he most convincing evidence for genetic influence on antisocial behavior comes from studies of adopted children who were separated at birth from their biological parents." These studies indicate that adoptive children whose biological parents were criminal are more likely to become criminal than children of adoptive parents who are criminal. Moreover, regardless of criminality of adoptive parent, children whose biological parent was criminal are more likely to become criminal (see also, Gottfredson & Hirschi, 1990:53-56). These findings have been interpreted to suggest that there is a genetic component predisposing some youth to engage in deviant activities.

The Disruption Paradigm

Disruption within the familial unit can stem from several sources. Arguing, ailing, mentally ill, or altogether absent parents can be difficult for children to cope with. Some of these stressors fall within the other paradigms summarized above. The most commonly studied form of disruption, however, is that resulting from the absence of one or both biological parents.

Some researchers have suggested that there exists a "two-tiered system of childrearing" (Sokol-Katz, Dunham, & Zimmerman, 1997:200; Tienda & Angel, 1982). One system consists of a two parent household, also termed, "intact homes." The other system is comprised of single-parent households where one individual (commonly the mother) is responsible for all aspects of parenting, also referred to as "broken homes." While the former system is the traditional structure, the latter is becoming increasingly common.[2] The effects of these changes in terms of adolescent development are still being explored.

Because rising crime rates have generally occurred concomitantly with changes in family composition in the

---

[2] Though the United States still has among the highest divorce rates, there is evidence that rates have begun to level off (see Goldstein, 1999).

previous two decades, concern has been raised that the two phenomena are in some way related. Indeed, research into the effect of family disruption on adolescent development is widespread (Haas, Farrington, Killias, & Sattar, 2004; Johnson, 1986; Juby & Farrington, 2001; Quensel et al., 2002; Rankin, 1983; Rebellon, 2002; Sampson & Laub, 1993; Wells & Rankin, 1991), and investigators have suggested that family disruption is more common in delinquent samples (Glueck & Gleuck, 1950). Additionally, the relationship between broken homes and delinquency has been supported by official and self-report studies and by several longitudinal studies (Juby & Farrington, 2001).

It has been estimated that approximately 40% of white children and 75% of African American children will experience parental separation or divorce before the age of 16 (Bray & Hetherington, 1993). Currently, there are about 12 million single-mother or single-father families in the United States, representing about 31% of all families (Fields & Casper, 2001). According to the United States Census Bureau (2000), about 27% of children under the age of 18 live in a one parent household. Of these, about 85% live with their mothers (U.S. Census Bureau, 2000). A variety of studies have demonstrated the negative consequences associated with families that have been disrupted by desertion, divorce, or death (Glueck & Glueck, 1962; Thornberry et al., 1999). For example, youth from one-parent families are more likely to use drugs (Wallace & Bachman, 1991) or engage in delinquent activities (Wells & Rankin, 1991) than youth from two-parent families. More specifically, Wells and Rankin (1991) found that youth residing in single-parent households were involved in 10-15% more delinquent activities than adolescents from intact homes. Rebellon (2002) presented evidence that Wells and Rankin's estimation may be low. Also, children who lived with one parent and his or her significant other (who was not related to youth) were more likely to join a gang in adolescence (Hill et al., 1999). Intuitively, children with only one parent often have more unsupervised time in which they could become involved in delinquent activities. As discussed above, parental supervision (or lack thereof) has been highly predictive of delinquent behavior (Vazsonyi & Flannery, 1997).

The negative effects of a single parent household also vary depending on with whom the youth is residing. Historically, much concern has been raised regarding separation of children from their mothers. As one theorist remarked:

> ...on the basis of this varied evidence it appears that there is a very strong case indeed for believing that prolonged separation of a child from his mother (or mother-substitute) during the first five years of life stands foremost among the causes of delinquent character development and persistent misbehavior (Bowlby, 1946, as quoted in Hirschi, 1969:86).

It has also been argued that young men who do not have the support of a "father figure" are more likely to engage in aberrant activities (Davies & Sinclair, 1971). In addition, Cantor (1982) found that the effects of a broken home on delinquency were stronger for boys than for girls.

Contrary to previous studies which found that attachment to mother was more important than attachment to father in reducing delinquency (i.e., Johnson, 1987; Krohn & Massey, 1980), Rankin and Kern (1994) argued that it is not the gender of the parent that is important, but the number of strong attachments. More specifically, children attached to both parents are less likely to be delinquent than youth attached to only one parent – even in families where both parents are still present (Rankin & Kern, 1994). Hirschi (1969:103), for example, maintained that the importance rests in the bond the youth maintains with the parent, and that "...the one parent family is virtually as efficient a delinquency-controlling institution as the two-parent family...." On the other hand, some researchers have suggested that the broken home creates fewer opportunities for strong attachment between the child and parent, and renders the child less likely to internalize familial norms (Elliott, Huizinga, & Ageton, 1985). Moreover, Rankin and Kern (1994) found that youth with attachment to two parents were less delinquent than youth who maintained a strong bond to one parent. Sokol-Katz and colleagues (1997:212) conclude that "it is possible to have a broken or reconstituted family that provides attachment and belief better than do some intact families, resulting in lower levels of delinquency."

Others have indicated that the presence of a stepparent places a child at risk because children are less likely to be strongly attached to nonbiological parents (Gottfredson & Hirschi, 1990; McCarthy, Gersten, & Langner, 1982; Rankin, 1983; Rebellon, 2002). Gottfredson and Hirschi (1990) argued that, all else being equal, a single, biological parent can be sufficient. Indeed, it is the ability of that parent to properly socialize his or her child such that self-control is developed that is important. These theorists asserted that one parent can accomplish this task as efficiently as two. Gottfredson and Hirschi (1990) also noted, however, that a single parent may find it more difficult to supervise his or her child at all times; yet, despite this disadvantage, they can succeed at properly socializing their children. In fact, Gottfredson and Hirschi further pointed out that a parent is not the only adult that can effectively socialize children; others from outside the home such as a grandparent or a mentor can also aid in the development of self-control.

Rankin (1983) also found a relationship between relatively minor antisocial behaviors (truancy, running away, vandalism, fighting) and family structure. Specifically, Rankin (1983) noted that homes in which both biological parents were absent were more likely to have a child who engaged in these activities compared to a home with only one absent parent. As Reiss (1951:199) argued, "It is generally agreed that children develop and maintain personal controls less readily when raised in a milieu other than the family of procreation."

Co-occurring Family Dysfunctions

Research cited on each of the family risk factors and correlates discussed above demonstrates that each is potentially hazardous by themselves. Often, however, adolescents are barraged with multiple risk factors over the course of their development. For example, Hirschi (1969) found that both prosocial and antisocial behaviors were highly correlated between parents. Similarly, Sampson and Laub (1993) found that father's deviance had a negative effect on mother's parenting. These findings suggest that youth who live with both parents may not necessarily be less at risk; if one parent demonstrates poor parenting skills or is deviant, it is very likely that the other may act similarly or is in some other way negatively impacted. Finally, Murray and Farrington (2005) examined the effect of parental imprisonment and note that the children of prisoners are extremely vulnerable to engage in delinquent behavior possibly due to the combination of disruption (being absent) and exposure to deviant parental beliefs. Reviewing much of the evidence available at the time regarding the above familial risk factors, Loeber and Stouthamer-Loeber (1986:92) conclude "...the risk of child problem behavior increases rapidly as the number of handicaps in the family increases."

Based on the preceding review, it is clear that the family is one of the most important socializing agents among developing adolescents. Youth are especially influenced by their parents and others within their family during their pre-adolescent years. By the time these youth enter adolescence, however, their attention tends to shift to other sources of influence (i.e. peers; Warr, 2002). A good familial environment early in life is crucial, because it can buffer youth from other risks that will eventually emerge. As explicated in this section, youth can be positively or negatively persuaded by what they learn within the family. Poor parenting predicts adolescent drug use, involvement in delinquency, and association with deviant gangs. Conversely, positive parenting protects youth from these and other negative influences. Proficient parenting can protect "...even biologically vulnerable and socioeconomically disadvantaged children" (Westman, 1996).

During an impressionable child's formative years, he or she is inundated with a host of positive and negative influences. The daunting task for each child is to sort through the good from the bad and make decisions based on experience, instruction, and intuition. Parents are instrumental in either directly or indirectly shaping these choices. As noted throughout this section, youth who fail to receive proper guidance or socialization are at an elevated risk to participate in delinquent behaviors. A small, yet significant proportion of these youth may engage in serious and/or violent behaviors. The following section will discuss the characteristics of these offenders.

SERIOUS, VIOLENT, AND EARLY JUVENILE OFFENDING

Serious and violent juvenile offenders pose the greatest challenges to the juvenile and criminal justice systems. These offenders are responsible for a disproportionate amount of deviance and, as a result, a significant amount of fiscal resources are exhausted due to the behavior of a small group of individuals (Farrington, 1987; Farrington & Loeber, 1998; Loeber, Farrington, & Waschbusch, 1998; Wolfgang, Figlio, & Selling, 1972). Most often, involvement in deviant activities peaks in post adolescence, between about ages 16 and 18 years (Farrington, 1986; Hirschi & Gottfredson, 1983). Others have noted, however, that criminal behavior can begin early in one's development and continue throughout the life-course (Sampson & Laub, 1993). Moreover, those youth who initiate offending at an early age (prior to age 14 years) are at an increased risk to become serious, violent, and/or chronic offenders (Moffitt, 1993).

Generally, juveniles who engage in Type I index offenses (homicide, rape, robbery, aggravated assault, burglary, theft over

$100, motor vehicle theft, arson) are characterized as serious and/or violent offenders. Additionally, this group of offenders is often involved in a number of other, less serious, offenses (Loeber & Farrington, 1998). Early starters are those youth who initiate offending prior to age 13 years (Loeber & Farrington, 2001). Serious offenders who begin at this early age are among the most at-risk to participate in illegal activities throughout their life course. Notably, the proportion of juveniles under the age of 13 who were arrested for a violent crime increased from 6% to 9% between 1980 and 2003 (Snyder & Sickmund, 2006). This section will discuss the characteristics of serious, violent, and early offenders, focusing on the causes and correlates of their behavior and what the future holds for such high-risk youth.

Age and Crime

Many researchers have argued that age of onset is an important factor in determining the nature of juvenile offending (Farrington, 1995; Glueck & Glueck, 1950; Sampson & Laub, 1993). Specifically, youth who initiate offending early are at an increased risk to have a prolonged career of offending that may continue into adulthood (Dishion, Capaldi, & Yoerger, 1999; Mazerolle, Brame, Paternoster, Piquero, & Dean, 2000; Patterson & Yoerger, 1999). Sampson and Laub (1993:135), for example, presented evidence that "...delinquent behavior in childhood has significant and substantial relationships with a wide range of adult criminal and deviant behaviors, including charges initiated by military personnel, interview-based reports of involvement in deviance and excessive drinking, and arrest by the police up to 30 years later."

Others, however, have argued that the age-crime curve is invariant across race and sex and has not changed in over one hundred years of criminological research (Hirschi & Gottfredson, 1983; Gottfredson & Hirschi, 1990). As such, consideration of early adolescent behavior is unnecessary. Many tests of this assertion have revealed, however, that age is important (Greenberg, 1985). For example, Steffensmeier, Allan, Harer, and Streifel (1989) reviewed the FBI's Uniform Crime Reports for the years 1940, 1960, and 1980 and discovered that the age-crime curve is in fact changing (the peak has steadily moved younger over the years). In short, while some traditional theorists have largely ignored the early years of child development, and others have argued that age is an unnecessary component of theoretical analysis, recent research questions these assumptions.

As a result of this debate, many researchers have proffered and tested developmental theories that account for stability and change of deviant tendencies throughout the life course (Patterson, DeBaryshe, & Ramsey, 1989; Thornberry, 2004). Two influential studies provided empirical support for this need (Blumstein et al., 1986; White, Moffitt, Earls, Robins, & Silva, 1990). In 1986, Blumstein and colleagues began investigating what they termed "career criminals." These individuals, they argued, represent a small minority in the population (5%), but are responsible for the majority of crimes that occurred (see also Wolfgang, Figlio, & Sellin, 1972). If society could successfully intervene with this small group, they reasoned, there would be a dramatic decrease in crime. Similarly, White and colleagues (1990) found that the best predictor of later adolescent offending (and consequently adult offending) was offending early in the life course (preschool).

Delinquency committed by children is becoming increasingly common. For example, in the United States, juvenile courts saw 33% more child delinquents in 1997 compared to 1988 (Loeber & Farrington, 2001). In Denver and Pittsburgh, approximately 10% of youth with a police record are either 11 or 12 years old (Espiritu, Huizinga, Crawford, & Loeber, 2001). Even though many children are not officially charged with a crime and referred to the juvenile court (Loeber & Farrington, 2001), approximately 1,300 persons between the ages of 10 and 12 were arrested for every 100,000 persons in this age group (Snyder & Sickmund, 2006). While this arrest rate represents a slight decline from 1980 (when the rate was 1,476 per 100,000), childhood offenders seem to be participating in more serious behaviors than ever before. To illustrate, the violent crime index arrest rate for juveniles between the ages of 10 and 12 increased by 27% (Snyder & Sickmund, 2006). These indicators suggest more attention ought to be directed toward childhood offenders as they appear to be engaging in more serious delinquent behaviors.

In general, causes of crime for early offenders typically occur within the individual (traits, biological or psychological – impulsivity, negative emotionality, constraint; Caspi et al., 1994; Snyder, 2001) or in the home (poor parenting), while correlates for later crime come from the environment (sociological explanations – peers, strain, etc). More specific examples will be detailed below.

Because crime tends to peak in late adolescence (property offenses earlier than personal offenses), many criminological theories focus on the adolescent years (or at least employ adolescent samples in testing their propositions). For example, differential association theory (Sutherland, Cressey, & Luckenbill, 1992) asserts that youth who associate with friends who have definitions favorable to the violation of the law will be more likely engage in delinquent activities than youth who associate with friends who have definitions unfavorable to the violation of the law (see also Matsueda, 1988). In addition, whether or not one becomes delinquent depends on the frequency, duration, intensity, and priority of these relationships (Sutherland et al., 1992). Because youth generally do not develop firm friendships until early adolescence – or later, and most of their influence during childhood comes from the home (Glueck & Glueck, 1950, Hirschi, 1969, Nye, 1958), differential association does not consider preadolescence as a time that influences future deviant activity (see also Thornberry, 1987).

Using structural equation modeling to test the applicability of the social development model (discussed below), Huang, Klosterman, Catalano, Hawkins, and Abbott (2001:98) found that "...youth who manifested violent behavior at age 13 were likely to persist in violent behavior at age 18, although antisocial socialization experiences continued to be an important mechanism for a significant amount of that persistence." Based on their findings, Huang and associates (2001:100) concluded that early intervention is best way to interrupt "antisocial socialization influences" from parents or peers that may be leading youth toward a delinquent path. Moreover, since prior violent behavior is one of the best predictors of future violence and aggression, early interventions that effectively control the behavior of children may result in long-term positive effects for years to come.

Using a nationally representative sample of youth (the National Youth Survey), Elliott (1994) found that 45% of respondents who began offending prior to age 11 years continued committing violent acts into their early 20's. Similarly, Moffitt (1993:678) pointed out that "(a)bout 6% of boys are first arrested by police as preteens...such early arrests are important because it is the best predictor of long-term recidivistic offending." Despite these concerns regarding the future outcomes of early offenders, many jurisdictions do not arrest or adjudicate such young children (Loeber & Farrington, 2001).

Many developmental researchers suggest that antisocial behavior is readily observable in very young children. For example, Moffitt (1993:675) maintained that "...it becomes obvious that manifestations of antisocial behavior emerge very early in the life course and remain present thereafter." Similarly, Patterson (1982:6) suggested that "...by the age of five most children in this society have learned most of the garden-variety aggressive behaviors employed by children." These behaviors may not be criminal or delinquent as defined by the law, but they are behaviors that may forecast future destructive behavior and therefore should result in some noninvasive preventative intervention efforts.

To summarize, early onset offenders persist longer and often engage in more serious offending for a number of reasons. First, early offending may be a sign that biological or psychological traits exist that put an individual at a disadvantage in the same environment where others may remain prosocial. Moreover, a disruptive family life further disadvantages these youth early in life. Second, early offending can result in cumulative disadvantages; that is, decisions made and actions taken early in life can affect opportunities later in life (Sampson & Laub, 1993). For example, youth who are labeled deviant may be treated differently by teachers who may relegate them to nonacademic tracks. This decision makes it difficult for youth to get accepted into college. Finally, antisocial behaviors can result in decreased bonding to conventional institutions such as the family, school, and work which can result in further deviance (Thornberry, 1987). For these reasons it is important to address the deviant behavior of pre-adolescent youth. If not corrected, these youth are at-risk to become serious and violent offenders.

Serious and Violent Juvenile Offenders

Increasing evidence is being accumulated which outlines the causes and correlates of serious and violent juvenile offending (Loeber & Farrington, 1998; OJJDP, 1998).[3] In a review of the development of (and paths leading toward) serious offending, Tolan and Gorman-Smith (1998:83) argued that "...violent and serious offenders can be differentiated from other offenders based on age of onset, presence of childhood behavior problems, and relative aggression level." Indeed, while many studies

---

[3] Currently, three longitudinal studies are underway in Denver, Pittsburgh, and Rochester which are designed to learn more about what causes (and is correlated with) serious delinquency (Browning, Huizinga, Loeber, & Thornberry, 1999). Preliminary results of this research indicate that family protective factors (adequate supervision, strong attachment, consistent discipline) are among the most important in promoting resilience.

indicated that the peak period of juvenile offending generally occurs between the ages of 14 and 17 years, serious offenders often report initiating offending between 7 and 14 years old (Loeber, Farrington, & Waschbusch, 1998). More specifically, in a comprehensive meta-analysis of predictors of serious and violent juvenile offending, Lipsey and Derzon (1998) found that after prior antisocial behavior between the ages of 6 and 11 years, male gender, low family socioeconomic status, and minority race were among the strongest predictors of serious and violent offending at age 15 to 25 years. Between 12 and 14 years old, previous antisocial behavior continues to be a good predictor of later serious/violent offending; additionally, associating with deviant peers and weak social ties also are strong predictors (Lipsey & Derzon, 1998). Interestingly, early substance use (6-11 years old) is a better predictor of future serious/violent offending than later substance use (12-14 years old).

As seriousness of offending increases, juveniles become involved in a variety of other antisocial activities (Loeber et al., 1998). Serious offenders use drugs and alcohol more frequently than nonoffenders; indeed, many excessive substance abusers are involved in serious crime (Huizinga & Jakob-Chein, 1998). Moreover, compared to nonoffenders, serious offenders are more aggressive, have more mental health and school problems, and are victimized more often (Huizinga & Jakob-Chein, 1998).

Hawkins, Laub, and Lauritsen (1998:109-42) identified a detailed list of malleable risk factors for youth violence that could be practically addressed with an appropriate intervention (see also Herrenkohl, Huang, et al., 2001:217). Notably, several such factors are embedded within the familial environment, including parental criminality, child maltreatment, poor parent-child relations and involvement, weak family bonding, parental attitudes toward violence, and separation from parents and early home leaving.

The more risk factors to which a youth is exposed, the greater the risk of future serious and/or violent offending. For example, aggressive children who live in a disorganized neighborhood with parents who are drug users are undoubtedly at a very high risk for future offending. Interventions ought to target specific risk factors in an effort to decrease this likelihood (Wasserman & Miller, 1998). It is also evident that specific risk factors can affect individuals differently depending on their developmental stage. For example, family-related risk factors may be more salient for young offenders (Tolan et al., 1995) while community and peer variables may become more important for older adolescents (Herrenkohl, Hawkins, et al., 2001). Finally, Guerra (1998:394) reminds researchers that "…it is important to distinguish risk factors useful for identification of populations (e.g., urban, economically disadvantaged), or subgroups of individuals (e.g., males), from risk factors to be targeted by an intervention (e.g., family management practices)."

Just because an adolescent has one (or a combination) of the above-described risk factors does not necessarily predict that he or she will become a serious offender. Similarly, just because an individual does not exhibit serious behavioral problems should not mean that he or she is unable to receive services that address identifiable risks. Teachers, parents, and other community members need to be aware of these risk factors so that preventative interventions can be employed when possible, *prior to initiation of offending*. Once serious offending is exhibited, however, immediate intervention is essential.

Serious and violent offenders are at a substantial risk for future offending. Moreover, youth who initiate offending early are at risk for future delinquency and criminality. As such, serious and violent offenders who begin between the ages of 10 and 13 years are among the most at-risk of all offenders (Loeber, 1982; Loeber & Farrington, 2001). Developing interventions that address their individual risk factors within multiple domains must be a priority if significant long-term reductions in crime are going to be realized.

SUMMARY

This preliminary chapter reviewed the extant literature concerning the main focuses of the current study. The reviewed body of work frames the present study by suggesting considerable utility in targeting the family relationships of serious, violent, and early juvenile offenders. As discussed above, there are several correlates of serious, violent, and early offending that originate from within the familial environment. Additionally, intervention efforts aimed at improving family relationships have proven successful among serious and violent offenders. These conclusions point to the utility of developing more widespread intervention approaches for serious and violent juvenile offenders that target familial relationships. The current study seeks to test this assertion.

The following chapter will reframe this discussion into contemporary theoretical perspectives. Several prominent criminological theories identify the importance of family relations and delinquency desistance. These ideas will help to shape the way in which interventions are developed and implemented. Indeed, the lack of evidence available regarding effective approaches to combat serious and violent juvenile delinquency is a social problem of significant import. This study seeks to fill this gap by theoretically and empirically examining the merit of an intervention approach that involves focusing on the family relationships of serious youthful offenders.

CHAPTER 2

The Theoretical Relationship between Family Relations and Delinquency

Many criminological theories recognize the important socializing role of parents within the familial domain. Nevertheless, theories often disagree as to the precise mechanism by which poor parenting contributes to deviant behaviors (Unnever et al., 2006). For example, social learning theorists acknowledge the importance of parents in conditioning, positive and negative reinforcement, modeling, and imitation (Akers, 1985, 1998; Bandura, 1973; Burgess & Akers, 1966). Social disorganization theorists also recognize the significance of the informal social control powers of families in neighborhoods (Bursik, 1988; Park & Burgess, 1924; Sampson, 1985; Sampson & Groves, 1989). Even strain theorists understand the negative outcomes associated with negative parent-child relationships (Agnew, 1992; Thaxton & Agnew, 2004). In addition to this tradition of familial influence being incorporated into traditional criminological theory, the family has taken a more prominent position in recent developmental theories of criminal behavior. For example, familial dysfunction can be a primary mechanism by which latent traits become manifested into deviant behavior.

Moreover, inattentive parents who do not take time to positively socialize their children may actually *cause* them to act out on impulses or negative feelings, thereby leading them toward a 'persistent' criminal career. Finally, family relationships are also incorporated into almost all of the most recent integrated theories (e.g., Agnew, 2005).

Despite the role parents and families play in the above-referenced theories, as a group, *control* theories most clearly acknowledge the importance of the parent-child relationship. Control theories emphasize "the prevention of crime through consequences painful to the individual" (Gottfredson & Hirschi, 1990:85). Historically, classical theorists focused on the legal sanctions that result from breaches of governmental law (e.g., imprisonment) (Beccaria, 1963). More recently, however, researchers have examined the effects of informal social control agents such as parents, neighbors, and others not affiliated with the formal justice system. The following sections describe this evolution, focusing on several social control theories that seek to explain crime and delinquency in terms of characteristics within the familial environment.

Several family attributes have been identified in theoretical models employed to explain deviance. Hirschi's (1969) social bond argues that youth who are strongly attached to their parents are less likely to engage in delinquent behavior. Patterson's (1980; 1982) coercion theory stresses the importance of direct supervision and discipline by parents in controlling the unwanted behaviors of their children. Catalano & Hawkins' social development model (1996) and Gottfredson and Hirschi's General Theory of Crime (1990) discuss the role of parents in socializing youth such that prosocial behavior is reinforced and proscribed behavior is disciplined. Finally, Sampson & Laub's (1993) age-graded theory of informal social control integrates elements of each of these perspectives. The following sections will review the theoretical underpinnings of, and empirical support for, each of these perspectives in terms of their focus on the family.

SOCIAL BOND

Social control theories focus on the ability of institutions to control the behavior of members of a particular society. Police act as formal social control agents operating on behalf of the greater community. Schools and churches also influence the behavior of their members. Similarly, families are recognized as a primary mechanism of informal social control. Early control theorists such as Reiss (1951) and Nye (1958) stressed the importance of the family. Moreover, many positivist researchers also have identified the role of the family in controlling latent traits and ultimately deviance (Glueck & Glueck, 1950). In 1969, Travis Hirschi explicated a version of social control theory that has been one of the most popular perspectives in research involving delinquency and the family (Rankin & Kern, 1994). This section will review the arguments of, and evidence for, Hirschi's approach.

As a control theorist, Hirschi (1969) assumed that individuals are inherently pleasure-seeking and therefore need to be 'controlled.' That is, left to their own devices and with no threat of reproval, all rational individuals will engage in deviant behavior to the extent that such behavior benefits them. As such, it is conformity rather than deviance that needs to be explained in criminological theorizing and empirical examination. Hirschi argued that conformity results when an individual is strongly bonded to conventional institutions such as the family, school, community, and church. His primary focus, however, concerned relations within the family. The social bond is comprised of four primary elements: attachment to significant others (notably parents), commitment to future goals (e.g., through education), involvement in conventional activities (e.g., extracurricular activities at school), and belief in the moral values of society (the internalization of conventional values).

In general, Hirschi's social control theory argues that parents control their children's behavior and buffer them from delinquency by forming strong social and emotional ties that bind children to their parents, and, by extension, to conventional order. Hirschi (1969:86) unequivocally described the relationship between parents and children in terms of their bond:

> As is well known, the emotional bond between the parent and the child presumably provides the bridge across which pass parental ideals and expectations. If the child is alienated from the parent, he will not learn or will have no feeling for moral rules, he will not develop an adequate conscience or superego.

Parents act not only as moral models, but coercive controllers if their children exhibit behavior that does not follow the mores, norms, and values of the family, or society at large. In short, parents are responsible for inculcating their children with positive morals and for strengthening these morals through positive reinforcement and caring correction so that children develop internal controls to govern their behavior when parents are absent. Hirschi argued that "(i)f the bond to the parent is weakened, the probability of delinquent behavior increases; if this bond is strengthened, the probability of delinquent behavior declines" (Hirschi, 1969:88). By and large, support exists for the hypothesis that increased parental attachment results in decreased delinquency (Cantor, 1982; Thaxton & Agnew, 2004; Wells & Rankin, 1988; Wiatrowski, Griswold, & Roberts, 1982).

There are several examples which help to illustrate the logic that an adolescent who is strongly bonded to his or her parents will engage in fewer delinquent acts than a weakly bonded child. First, a youth who is well bonded to a parent will likely spend more time with that parent which may result in closer direct supervision by that parent and thus fewer opportunities for deviant behavior. Because parents cannot supervise their children all of the time, the emotional bond between parent and child can act to control the child's actions even when the parent is not present, a process known as "virtual supervision" (Cernkovich & Giordano, 1987; Hirschi, 1969). Children who perceive that their parents do not know where they are or what they are doing are more likely to report involvement in deviance (Hirschi, 1969:89). Junger & Marshall (1997), for example, found that low virtual supervision was significantly related to self-reported delinquency in a sample of ethnically diverse lower-class youth.

Because virtual supervision is concerned with indirect control, Hirschi argued that its effectiveness is more a function of intimacy of communication than supervision. That is, youth who share their experiences with their parents on a regular basis are more likely to consider the response of their parents before engaging in proscribed activities. Combined with other measures of communication (e.g., "Do you share your thoughts and feelings with your mother/father?"), virtual supervision was again highly predictive of self-reported delinquency (that is, youth with more intimacy of communication were less likely to report involvement in delinquency; Hirschi, 1969).

Strong ties to parents inhibit delinquency because children fear unfavorable responses from parents if antisocial behaviors ever become known. More specifically, youth who are psychologically attached will fear the emotional damage caused by the disobedience (as opposed to actual physical punishment). These ideas also have been termed "stakes in conformity" (Toby, 1957); attached individuals have a "stake" in conforming to societal expectations – namely, parental approval.

While Hirschi (1969) devoted most of his attention to discussing the effects of a strong bond to *conventional* parents (that is, prosocial and law-abiding), he acknowledged the difficulty in this theory when children are born to deviant parents. He concludes, nonetheless, that youth who are firmly attached, even to deviant parents, will be less likely to engage in deviance than those weakly attached to the same type of parents. Hirschi suggests that even if parents are involved in criminal activities or hold favorable definitions to deviance, they would do their best to avoid passing those ideals and behaviors on to their children. In the eyes of the child, then, parents act as a proxy for a conventional law-abiding citizen.

While social learning theory suggests that youth who associate with deviant others are more likely to engage in deviance than those who do not (Akers, 1985, 1998; also referred to as cultural deviance theories), Hirschi (1969) contended that delinquent peers will become salient only if the attachment to parents is weak. Hirschi's (1969:100) data support this claim; regardless of the number of delinquent friends with whom a youth associates, children who were more attached to their father were less likely to engage in delinquent behavior.

Using data from the Richmond Youth Survey—a random sample of approximately 4,000 youth from the San Francisco-Oakland, California metropolitan area—Hirschi presented initial empirical support for many components of his theory. Others, too, have provided empirical support for Hirschi's social control theory (Cernkovich, 1978; Cernkovich & Giordano, 1987, 1992; Costello & Vowell, 1999; Fagan & Wexler, 1987; Kempf, 1993; Sokol-Katz et al, 1997; Wiatrowski et al., 1981). For example, Alarid, Burton Jr., and Cullen (2000) tested the efficacy of social control theory on a sample of approximately 1,100 incarcerated felons and concluded that Hirschi's social bonding theory is a "general" theory in the sense that it explained variation in a variety of deviance (general crime scale, drug, property, and violent subscales) and had similar effects among males and females.

Similarly, Erickson, Crosnoe, and Dornbusch (2000) empirically tested the hypothesis that strong social bonds to parents reduce the likelihood of youth associating with deviant peers (see also Ingram et al., 2006; Warr, 2005). They found that youth who reported strong ties to parents were significantly less likely to have close friends who frequently participated in delinquent activities (Erickson et al., 2000). This finding is especially useful because researchers actually asked the youths' friends about their involvement in deviance, thus avoiding the problem of youth reporting their own behavior as that of their peers. Parental attachment (measured as a scale representing questions such as: "I try to have the same opinion as my parents" and "My parents spend time just talking with me") and supervision (a scale including: "How much do your parents really know your friends?" and "How much do your parents know about what you do with your free time?") and other social control variables accounted for 18% of the variation in delinquent peer associations (Erickson et al., 2000). Erickson and colleagues (2000:420) concluded that "(a)dolescents who experience strong social attachments, commitments, and involvements are less likely to jeopardize personal relationships and accomplishments by associating with peers who support and engage in deviance." In short, strong attachment to parents can insulate adolescents from other criminogenic factors and must therefore be considered in any comprehensive delinquency prevention program.

Dornbusch, Erickson, Laird, and Wong (2001) empirically tested the power of familial attachment to reduce the frequency, prevalence, and intensity of cigarette smoking, alcohol use, marijuana use, delinquency, and violent behavior among a nationally representative sample of approximately 13,000 7th through 12th grade students. They found that familial attachment acted as a protective factor in that youth who were more strongly attached were significantly less likely to report all forms of deviance (Dornbusch et al., 2001). Moreover, these relationships held across diverse communities (different levels of economic deprivation), and ethnicities, as well as across gender. A unique attribute of this study was the utilization of parental reports of attachment, supplementing those of the youthful respondent. Indeed, the parental report of attachment was "the measure most often significantly associated with reductions in deviance..." (Dornbusch et al., 2001: 417),

Interestingly, Anderson, Holmes, and Ostresh (1999) found gender differences in the relationship between attachment and delinquency (see also Cernkovich & Giordano, 1987). In a sample of incarcerated delinquents in Wyoming, they found that attachment to parents reduced the severity of delinquent behavior among boys while attachment to school and peers had the same effect for girls. That is, girls in this study appeared to be more affected by school and peers than by parents. This research replicated other studies (for example, Cantor, 1982) which found that even though girls tended to be more strongly attached to their parents in general, intensity of attachment had a greater delinquency-reducing effect among boys.

May, Vartanian, and Virgo (2002) investigated the effect of parental attachment and supervision on fear of crime among incarcerated adolescents and found mixed results. First, parental supervision was significantly related to fear of victimization (highly supervised youth were more likely to fear victimization), yet respondents were less likely to acknowledge that they could be at risk of crime victimization (May et al., 2002). Second, parental attachment had no significant effect on an adolescent's fear of crime. May and colleagues (2002) conclude, therefore, that youth who are highly supervised may be "sheltered" from crime yet not empowered with strategies to deal with potential situations that might arise.

Others, however, have questioned Hirschi's assertions (Matsueda, 1982). For example, Greenberg (1999) reanalyzed the Richmond Youth Survey and found only weak support for social control theory. Another problem with Hirschi's analysis, Greenberg (1999) argues, is that Hirschi was assessing the relationship between the level of social bond at the time of the interview and previous delinquency. Using this interpretation, delinquent behavior may actually predict the level of social bond because the temporal ordering is not correctly specified (Thornberry, 1987).

As evidenced by this review, much research has been conducted concerning Hirschi's (1969) social control theory and the link between family relationships and adolescent deviance. Despite this wealth of knowledge, however, few concrete conclusions have emerged. A few generalizations can be offered, based on the preponderance of the evidence. First,

Hirschi's social bonding theory is an important contribution to the understanding of deviant behavior. Weaknesses that have been cited are reconcilable, and researchers continue to test and refine the perspective so as to produce a more comprehensive theoretical model. Second, the family is one of the most important institutions in an adolescent's life and therefore must be considered in any model attempting to explain antisocial behavior. Hirschi provides a starting point from which researchers can continue exploring the complex relationships that occur within the family and how they affect delinquent involvement.

SOCIAL DEVELOPMENT MODEL

The social development model integrates multiple theories (control, learning, and differential association) and stresses the importance of risk and protective factors in multiple social domains (Catalano & Hawkins, 1996). Familial risk factors include: "...family history of drug abuse or crime, poor family management practices, family conflict, low family bonding, and parental permissiveness..." (Catalano & Hawkins, 1996:152). Familial protective factors include: "...family cohesion and warmth or bonding during childhood..." (Catalano & Hawkins, 1996:153).

Drawing from differential association theory, the social development model acknowledges that an individual's behavior is largely determined by the behavior of those with whom he or she associates. Consistent with control theory, individuals who have strong social bonds to prosocial others are inhibited from engaging in deviant behavior for fear of damaging that relationship. The social development model views the bond to the family as critical in the development of bonds to other social institutions (Hawkins, Catalano, Jones, & Fine, 1987). Finally, akin to learning theory, the social development model argues that behaviors are learned from others within intimate settings and involve both imitation and reinforcement. In short, youth are socialized within primary groups (e.g., family, peers, school) to engage in either prosocial or antisocial ways.

The social development model seeks to explain a wide variety of antisocial behaviors across the life course, but focuses on the influence of risk and protective factors during four developmental periods: preschool, elementary school, middle school, and high school. Transitions between each of these periods are also important stages of development. The model "hypothesizes that children learn patterns of behavior, whether prosocial or antisocial, from the socializing agents of family, school, religious and other community institutions and their peers" (Huang et al., 2001:77). Moreover, it specifies multiple pathways to delinquency within multiple developmental periods.

Using structural equation modeling, Huang and colleagues (2001) found that the social development model was an acceptable fit to the Social Development Project sample. They found that youth who developed rewarding relationships with antisocial others in middle school were more likely to engage in substance use and violent behavior later. Interestingly, they also found that antisocial socialization (opportunities, involvement, and rewards) was more salient than simple bonds (attachment and belief) to antisocial others. This finding is consistent with Hirschi's (1969) argument that an individual who has a strong bond to antisocial others will not necessarily be negatively influenced by their behavior.

In another examination of the social development model, Herrenkohl and associates (2001) found that the socialization processes leading to violence at age 18 were the same for youth who initiated offending in childhood (10-11) or early adolescence (12-16). The researchers suggest that this finding calls into question the assertions of many who argue that childhood offenders are categorically different from adolescent initiators (Moffitt, 1993). This conclusion is itself questionable, considering their operationalization of childhood offending. It could be argued that a 12 or even 13 year old offender is still a childhood offender (or an early starter). Nevertheless,

Herrenkohl and associates (2001) find support for the social development model's hypothesis, which argues that socialization within antisocial circles will lead to antisocial behaviors, especially when that behavior is reinforced. These researchers conclude, then, that parenting skills training coupled with adolescent social skills training appears to be a theoretically promising approach to altering children's socialization mechanisms and behaviors (Herrenkohl et al., 2001). Specifically, they advocate that parent training should focus on "age-appropriate discipline strategies and monitoring" (Herrenkohl et al., 2001:60).

Ayers and colleagues (1999) found that several social development model constructs were significantly related to delinquency desistance (e.g., higher social skills, higher grades, more conventional peer associations, more commitment to school, more belief in moral order). Important for the purposes of the current study, these researchers also found that females were more bonded to their families at age 12-13 and that this bond was related to desistance for females but not males. They conclude that interventions aimed at improving parent-child interactions may be more successful among females at this age, and that such approaches may need to begin earlier to be successful with male offenders (Ayers et al., 1999).

One limitation to the above-referenced tests of the social development model is that most were conducted using the same data (data from the Seattle Social Development Project). To ensure that the hypothesized relationships occur in a variety of settings, researchers must begin to test the social development model on other samples (Fleming, Catalano, Oxford, & Harachi, 2002).

The social development model is an ideal theoretical framework from which to develop intervention approaches because it identifies specific risk and protective factors that can be targeted. The social development model acknowledges the inseparability of multiple domains, and the need to address juvenile delinquency from within multiple spheres.

Additionally, this perspective also proposes that interventions should increase opportunities for prosocial involvement, enhance the child's social skills, and ensure consistent and reasonable rewards and punishments for prosocial and proscribed behaviors (Hawkins et al., 1987).

The social development model integrates much of the previous theoretical work that focuses on the process of socialization, particularly the influence of the family in this process. The model differs from traditional social control theory by arguing that youth who are strongly bonded to antisocial others are at risk for engaging in delinquent behavior. Moreover, it includes elements of social learning and differential association theories which identify the power of others to influence one's behavior. Finally, similar to other control theories, the social development model assumes that individuals are rational actors who are willing to engage in a variety of behaviors (prosocial and antisocial) to the extent that their own pleasure is maximized and pain minimized.

For the purposes of the current study, it is clear that the family firmly remains a central tenet in the socialization process. Improper socialization by the family places adolescents at an elevated risk for engaging in antisocial activities. Moreover, parents who are involved in criminal activities may reinforce the acceptability of these activities to their children. In short, if the process by which an early adolescent delinquent becomes an adult criminal is to be effectively interrupted, program administrators must remain cognizant of the risk and protective factors associated with the family environment.

COERCION THEORY

Like other variations of control theory, coercion theory is concerned with the mechanisms by which adolescents refrain from engaging in delinquency (Patterson, 1980, 1982). Coercion theory maintains that parents are responsible for supervising and controlling the behavior of their children. Patterson (1980), however, argued that coercion theory is a reformulation of social learning theory in that children view deviance as normative because their parents either tolerate or are incapable of addressing the child's deviant behavior. As such, unskilled parenting can result in increased risk for child to become involved in continued delinquent behavior. Patterson (1980:81) presented an explicit set of skills parents can employ to encourage prosocial development:

> (a) notice what the child is doing; (b) monitor it over long periods; (c) model social skill behavior; (d) clearly state house rules; (e) consistently provide sane punishments for transgressions; (f) provide reinforcement for conformity; and (g) negotiate disagreements so that conflicts and crises do not escalate.

Coercion theory is "...a set of statements about pain-control techniques employed by one or both members of a dyad" (Patterson, 1982:6). Any member of a group can apply coercion strategies. For example, children behave in certain ways to achieve an intended result (e.g., toddlers cry to attain the attention of a parent). Also, parents are impelled to respond to the behavior of their children (e.g., punish or ignore forbidden behaviors). Because coercion theory predicts a reciprocal relationship between members of the dyad, it does not necessarily provide insight as to causality. That is, did ineffective parenting cause the child to turn toward deviance, or did the deviant child cause the parent to question his or her ability to parent effectively? Patterson suggests that this dialectic relationship likely occurs as a result of both processes (see also Thornberry, 1987). "In families of antisocial children some parental 'neuroses' can be thought of as the outcome or a process rather than its cause" (Patterson, 1982:11).

Patterson's model differs from Hirschi's (1969) conception of social control in that Patterson is concerned largely with the direct inhibiting properties of parental supervision, whereas Hirschi proposed that the affective relationship between parent and child (social bond) indirectly controls behavior (Sampson & Laub, 1993). That is, according to Patterson, children will refrain from engaging in delinquent activities because their parents are watching or will find out about such behaviors, resulting in some form of negative stimuli (punishment). According to Hirschi (1969), children will refrain from engaging in anti-social activities for fear of damaging their relationship with prosocial institutions (such as the family) if caught (see also Thornberry, 1987). Sampson and Laub (1993) point out, however, that these two processes are likely correlated; that is, parents who effectively supervise their children also typically have well-developed affective ties with them.

Patterson (1980:83) further maintained that "...parents reinforce and punish in a manner isomorphic with their own established hierarchy of social behavior and values. That is, they *support* what *they themselves actually do.*" Additionally, Patterson noted that while parents themselves may not be criminals or engage in many criminal activities, they do, however, often deliberately ignore antisocial behavior when it occurs in their children. Parents either do not believe others when they say that their children behaved in certain ways, or are unprepared to prosocially discipline their child effectively.

Coercion theory argues that the two most important aspects of effective parenting are monitoring and discipline. According to coercion theory, children do not simply grow out of antisocial behavior; they will continue engaging in proscribed activities unless adequately punished. "Antisocial acts that are not punished tend to persist. Parents of stealers do not track; they do not punish; and they do not care" (Patterson, 1980:89). Parents who are incapable or unwilling to consistently discipline their children for engaging in deviant activities are implicitly endorsing the behavior. What is needed, then, is comprehensive training to teach parents how to authoritatively manage antisocial behavior by their children. Patterson (1980:77) argues that

"...what is necessary is that the family directly punish, nonphysically, the deviant acts and concentrate on teaching prosocial competing responses." Patterson (1980) found that parents who participated in skills training were able to significantly decrease the frequency of stealing among their children.

Coercion theory assumes that aggression in families is not merely the aggregation of several "fortuitous events" (Patterson, 1982:12). Moreover, while many researchers focus only on extreme forms of aggression, Patterson (1982) suggests that minor, relatively harmless acts (such as teasing and disciplining) can escalate into more serious forms of aggression (hitting).

Patterson proffers a coercion theory that attempts to elucidate the didactic relationship between parent and child. In short, like other control theories, the theory predicts that ineffective child rearing (specifically, poor monitoring and/or discipline) will result in children who are at risk of engaging in delinquent behavior. Youth who perceive that they are not being treated fairly will foreclose on childhood by engaging in "adult-like" deviant behaviors (e.g., smoking, drinking, stealing) to demonstrate to others that they are "grown-up" (see also Moffitt, 1993). While the theoretical analysis has merit, it has not been empirically scrutinized. Patterson's insistence upon the significance of parenting skills in delinquency desistance, however, is important and therefore relevant to the present study.

GENERAL THEORY OF CRIME – SELF-CONTROL

Gottfredson and Hirschi (1990) detailed a general theory of crime that holds low self-control as the primary variable which predicts crime, delinquency, and other analogous undesirable outcomes. They also assert that the propensity to engage in deviant behavior remains stable over time; as a result, differences in actual involvement in crime can be attributed to population heterogeneity and variation in opportunity to engage in illicit activities. In short, Gottfredson and Hirschi (1990:89)

"...suggest that high self-control effectively reduces the possibility of crime—that is, those possessing it will be substantially less likely at all periods of life to engage in criminal acts." In other words, individuals with low self-control will always be at risk for engaging in some behavior that may be harmful to others (whether legally prohibited or not). Gottfredson and Hirschi (1990:90) further argue that "...people who lack self-control will tend to be impulsive, insensitive, physical (as opposed to mental), risk-taking, short-sighted, and nonverbal, and they will tend therefore to engage in criminal and analogous acts."

While many criminologists have criticized Gottfredson and Hirschi's hypothesis (Akers, 1991; Geis, 2000; Marcus, 2004), their analysis can be informative as to how best to address deviant behavior. Indeed, despite initial disparagement, impressive empirical support has emerged for their theory (Burton, Cullen, Evans, Alarid, & Dunaway, 1998; Grasmick, Tittle, Bursik, & Arneklev, 1993; Junger & Tremblay, 1999; LaGrange & Silverman, 1999; Paternoster & Brame, 1998; Pratt & Cullen, 2000). Their ideas regarding the relationship between family socialization and involvement in delinquency are more instructive, but less often empirically tested (Hay, 2001; Lynskey, Winfree, Jr., Esbensen, & Clason, 2000; Wright & Beaver, 2005). Gottfredson and Hirschi (1990) suggested that the relationship between parenting and delinquency is mediated by self-control. "In our view, the origins of criminality of low self-control are to be found in the first six or eight years of life, during which time the child remains under the control and supervision of the family or a familial institution" (Gottfredson & Hirschi, 1990:272).

Gottfredson and Hirschi's (1990) general theory of crime acknowledges the primary role parents play in socializing their children to develop strong self-control: "...[S]elf-control differences seem primarily attributable to family socialization practices" (Gottfredson & Hirschi, 1990:107). Indeed, others have found that parental monitoring and disciplining techniques significantly predict levels of self-control, which in turn is related to delinquency (Hay, 2001; Lynskey, Winfree, Esbensen, & Clason, 2000; Polakowski, 1994; Pratt, Turner, & Piquero, 2004; Unnever, Cullen, & Pratt, 2003). The mediating role of self-control in Hay's (2001) study, however, was not as clear. Parents play a crucial role in that self-control is developed (almost exclusively in the family) in the first few years and remains relatively stable across the life course (Gottfredson & Hirschi, 1990; Nagin & Paternoster, 1991). If parents fail to adequately socialize their children such that self-control is not fully developed, then they may be at a greater risk for delinquency.

Gottfredson and Hirschi (1990:97) maintain that "the major 'cause' of low self-control thus appears to be ineffective child-rearing." Further, similar to coercion theory, they argue that three conditions represent proper child-rearing: "someone must (1) monitor the child's behavior; (2) recognize deviant behavior when it occurs; and (3) punish such behavior" (p. 97). Gottfredson and Hirschi point out that these conditions are rarely intentionally violated by parents, but that parents often implicitly fail to adequately socialize their children in one of four ways, which can result in underdeveloped self-control. First, some parents, whether deliberately of not, do not properly care for their children. Second, even caring parents may fail to adequately supervise their children, so that deviant behavior goes unnoticed and unpunished. Third, caring and attentive parents may not see anything wrong with the types of behaviors in which the child is engaging. Finally, even if parents are caring, attentive, and cognizant of the prosocial and antisocial activities in which their child is involved, they may be unable or unwilling to punish their children for the deviant behaviors. Any of these conditions may result in the failure of children to develop strong self-control early in life.

Generally, parents cannot deliberately train their children to have low self-control, thereby increasing their delinquency. It is the lack of involvement such as that described above that can result in underdeveloped self-control. Gottfredson and Hirschi (1990:94-5) argue this point: "One thing is, however, clear: low self-control is not produced by training, tutelage, or socialization. As a matter of fact, all of the characteristics associated with low self-control tend to show themselves in the absence of nurturance, discipline, or training." Neglect in parental responsibilities may result in a child who has not firmly developed self-control and as a result is at a risk for engaging in deviant activities. Gottfredson and Hirschi's (1990:101) general theory "...assumes criminality is not something the parents have to work to produce; on the contrary, it assumes that criminality is something they have to work to avoid."

Other research has examined the extent to which self-control is genetically determined and not necessarily created exclusively through specific parenting practices. Wright and Beaver (2005) analyzed a random sample of 1,000 youth and initially found support for the relationship between parenting and self-control. Results from a twin subsample (n=310), however, indicated that genetic influences ostensibly accounted for much of the variation in levels of self-control as a number of parenting measures failed to remain statistically significant. Wright and Beaver conclude that more sophisticated methods are necessary to better understand the complex relationship between parenting and self-control while accounting for genetic or other biological influences.

The idea that self-control is an important mechanism by which criminal and delinquent tendencies are restrained is not new. Approximately fifty years ago, Reiss (1951) and Nye (1958) also recognized the power of the individual to control his or her own behavior. Reiss's concept of personal controls and Nye's conception of internalized controls represent the same force that Gottfredson and Hirschi extol in their general theory. Moreover, even Reiss (1951:198) recognized the role of families and other "primary groups" in the development of "personal controls" among adolescents:

Primary groups are the basic institutions for the development of personal controls and the exercise of social control over the child....Delinquency and delinquent recidivism may be viewed as a consequence of the failure of primary groups to provide the child with appropriate non-delinquent social roles and to exercise social control over the child so these roles are accepted or submitted to in accord with needs.

In contrast to Hirschi's (1969) social bond theory which argues that a strong bond to any institution should reduce the likelihood of offending, Reiss (1951) suggests that parents must model prosocial attitudes and behaviors for their children to internalize and imitate. This earlier conceptualization of control theory is also evident in the social development model discussed above (Catalano & Hawkins, 1996).

Even though Gottfredson and Hirschi's (1990) general theory of crime ostensibly indicates that the development of self-control is the only way to reduce criminality, they firmly reject the theory's utility in intervention development: "...all indications are that such teaching is highly unlikely to be effective unless it comes very early in development" (1990:269). These theorists maintain that socialization must occur prior to that age at which a child is able to manifest low self-control in delinquent ways (e.g., prior to age 8 years). Accordingly, Gottfredson and Hirschi promote early prevention efforts that train children to delay gratification. But what is to be done about older children and adolescents whose parents were incapable of providing these lessons? The implications of their perspective are less clear for older populations of offenders.

While Gottfredson and Hirschi (1990) did not suggest that their theory can aid in the development of effective interventions for offending populations, it is possible that their analysis can inform intervention efforts. If they are correct in asserting that self-control is the latent trait responsible for criminality (and many tests of the general theory have provided some supportive evidence), attempts to develop self-control in an intervention context may be worth pursuing. Also following their analysis, the most effective way to develop self-control is from within the family context. As such, interventions ought to focus on the family; more specifically, interventions may be more effective if they train parents in child-rearing strategies and positive reinforcement, as well as efficient supervision and monitoring.

AGE-GRADED THEORY OF INFORMAL SOCIAL CONTROL

Control theorists have long recognized that disapproval by loved ones is as powerful a sanction as any formal legal threat (Gottfredson & Hirschi, 1990). As such, many researchers have explored the relationship between informal social control agents such as families and peer groups in the management of crime and deviance. One such theoretical perspective is Sampson and Laub's (1993) age-graded theory of informal social control. Sampson and Laub's (1993) approach began from a traditional social control perspective in that a weakened bond to society can result in deviant behavior (Durkheim, 1951; Hirschi, 1969; Kornhauser, 1978). Sampson and Laub (1993:68) "...combined the central ideas of social control and coercion theory along with the notion of reintegrative shaming into a unified model of informal family social control that focuses on three dimensions—discipline, supervision, and attachment." These scholars began with the view that social control is "...the capacity of a social group to regulate itself according to desired principles and values, and hence to make norms and rules effective" (Sampson & Laub, 1993:18).

According to Sampson & Laub (1993), there are several ways in which the family promotes or reduces delinquency. If turning points do not occur at developmentally normal stages (e.g., graduation in late teens, followed by college, military or job experiences in the early twenties, and marriage and children shortly thereafter), individuals could be 'turned' toward delinquent paths. For example, adolescents who are kicked out of their homes for inappropriate behavior may sever familial ties too early. This may result in the over-reliance on peers for emotional and financial support. If prosocial friends are unavailable to youths, deviant peers will supplant the family as the important reference group.

Sampson & Laub (1993, 1995) acknowledged the effects of the family across the life course. Their theory of informal social control is probably the best example of a perspective that considers the role of the family over the entire life course. For example, the family is an important buffer from crime both as a child and adult; parents supervise their children while spouses and children are incentives for adults to remain crime-free. Additionally, Sampson and Laub (1993) provided an age-graded theory that accounts for stability and change throughout the life course, and the family is the primary mechanism of informal social control at several stages. As an age-graded theory, Sampson and Laub recognized the different ways in which the family can be involved in delinquency prevention at various stages of development. First, as youth develop, parents socialize their children to ingrain in them their own set of norms, values, and beliefs. Parents also reinforce positive behavior while condemning negative behaviors. Moreover, parents supervise their children so that they are able teach life lessons at appropriate times. During adolescence, however, parental influence begins to wane. Peers become more important during this stage (Elliott, Huizinga, & Ageton, 1985; Warr, 2002), and parents need to rely on the values that they have instilled in their children to that point. Sampson and Laub (1993:97) also maintain, however, that "...delinquency in adolescence is explained largely by exogenous family factors that also occur in adolescence," such as supervision and effective socialization.

In the early twenties, the family once again returns as the prominent protective factor in keeping individuals from engaging in criminal activities. As individuals marry and have children of their own, they develop stakes in conformity (Toby

1957) or social capital (Coleman, 1988) that will continue to keep them from engaging in deviant activities. In brief, Sampson and Laub (1993:141) argue, "...social ties are important insofar as they create interdependent systems of obligation and restraint that impose significant costs for translating criminal propensities into action." Similarly, Farrington (1986:189) suggests that "the age crime curve probably reflects decreasing parental controls, a peaking of peer influence in the teenage years, and then increasing family and community controls with age."

Sampson and Laub (1993:7) argued three main points regarding the relationship between family and delinquency/crime across the life course:

> (1) structural context mediated by informal family and school social controls explains delinquency in childhood and adolescence; (2) in turn, there is continuity in antisocial behavior from childhood through adulthood in a variety of life domains; and (3) informal social bonds in adulthood to family and employment explain changes in criminality over the life span despite early childhood propensities.

Sampson & Laub (1993) also considered the family in the continuity and change of criminality. They recognize specific 'turning points' and how they may result in an individual changing his or her trajectory (long term pathway or line of development) over time. For example, removal of one parent by death or divorce may negatively affect a youth. He or she may attempt to escape emotional pain by turning to deviant peers or illicit substances. Conversely, if the parent who was removed was abusing the child or in some other way disrupting the familial environment, strain may be lifted and the youth may return to a prosocial trajectory.

Transitions that occur (marriage, first job, arrest) can positively or negatively redirect the trajectory on which an individual appears to be headed. There is a developmentally appropriate progression of transitions that most individuals experience which often results in normative development. Summarizing the life-course perspective, Sampson and Laub (1993:8) note that "...life course analyses are often characterized by a focus on the duration, timing, and ordering of major life events and their consequences for later social development." As discussed above, many individuals transition into high school, then graduate from high school, enter the workforce, get married, then have children. Individuals who experience these events out of developmental order (e.g., having children before graduating high school) are at increased risk for engaging in criminal behaviors. To be sure, some delinquency, if minor and engaged in during adolescence (e.g., truancy, fighting, minor theft), is common and considered developmentally appropriate (Moffitt, 1993). Early or prolonged involvement in these behaviors, however, is a potent risk factor for future delinquency (see discussion of early offenders in Chapter 1).

Sampson and Laub's approach is unique in that it is a developmental perspective that extends beyond childhood and adolescence and considers the importance of informal social control mechanisms into adulthood. More specifically, these theorists maintained that different formal and informal social control institutions can influence individuals differently at different ages. Additionally, Sampson and Laub (1993:19) argued that "...informal social controls derived from the family (for example, consistent use of discipline, monitoring, and attachment) and school (for instance, attachment to school) mediate the effects of both individual and structural background variables."

Sampson and Laub (1993:246) further contend that structural context (disorganization, disadvantage, etc) is mediated by informal family social controls:

It is our view that family and school processes of informal social control provide the key causal explanation of delinquency in childhood and adolescence. Structural background characteristics are important in terms of their effects on informal family and school processes, but these same characteristics have little direct influence on delinquency.

That is, youth residing in a poor neighborhood who regularly witness crime and deviance may be buffered from the deleterious effects of that environment if effectively controlled by their parents (Patchin, Huebner, McCluskey, Varano, & Bynum, 2006). Moreover, underlying traits that may predispose an individual to deviance (e.g., low self-control) can be adequately handled through a strong bond to the family. As such, living in a disadvantaged neighborhood may be a risk factor only for youths who also do not have competent parents (in contrast see Brooks-Gunn et al., 1993).

THEORY TO PRACTICE: FAMILY-FOCUSED INTERVENTIONS

Based on the theoretical perspectives reviewed above, it can be deduced that family relationships are a malleable factor that can be adequately addressed in an intervention context. Moreover, if a child does not have a strong, positive relationship with his or her parent(s), other intervention efforts may prove ineffective. The intervention may be a turning point for the family (both for parent and child), as children learn that there are consequences for their behavior and parents learn that their children are "out of control." As such, simply being ordered to participate in an intervention may improve family relations and therefore reduce offending. Alternatively, however, interventions may need to specifically target familial processes early in order to prime the family for other programming (e.g., drug treatment, life skills).

Reviews have suggested that family interventions are often more effective than non-family interventions (Dowden & Andrews, 2003; Latimer, 2001; Perkins-Dock, 2001). Moreover,

Kazdin (1987) argued that family interventions hold the most promise for the treatment of Conduct Disorder in children and adolescents. Finally, parent-focused interventions implemented at home or in other community locations also tend to be very successful (Burns et al., 2003).

A notable attribute of effective family-centered interventions is the focus on multiple domains. Indeed, a wealth of knowledge suggests that individually focused programs, by themselves, do little to effectively prevent future crime. As discussed at length, juvenile delinquency is a multiply-determined phenomena resulting from the convergence of risk factors in the absence of effective protective factors. As such, several agencies (e.g., police, mental health, school, court) must coordinate efforts in order to provide a "wraparound" model whereby all individual and familial needs are addressed. The challenge, then, is to develop a program that is comprehensive enough to address myriad risk and protective factors but that is easily implemented in diverse settings (i.e., ecologically valid). In short, serious juvenile offenders require theoretically grounded, comprehensive, multimodal interventions that address specific risk and protective factors within a flexible framework (Black, Howard, Kim, & Ricardo, 1998).

SUMMARY

Social control theories are among the most empirically supported theories in criminology (Akers, 2000). Even self-control (fostered by parents) has been identified and empirically supported as a leading correlate of crime. Specific tests of developmental theories such as Sampson & Laub's (1993) age-graded theory of informal social control are steadily emerging. In many ways, Sampson and Laub's theory attempts to reconcile the inherent differences between traditional control theory (Hirschi, 1969) and contemporary self-control theory (Gottfredson & Hirschi, 1990). That is, individual differences in early childhood predispositions (low self-control) are mediated by social structural influences (family).   Moreover, these relationships, and by extension criminality, can at the same time remain relatively stable over time (exhibit homotypic continuity) or change dramatically (see also Loeber, 1982; Moffitt, 1993; Olweus, 1979).   Indeed, Gottfredson and Hirschi (1990) and Sampson and Laub (1993:17) are in agreement in that "...the tendency of individuals to remain relatively stable over time on the dimension of deviance points to the early life course—especially family socialization and child rearing—as a key causal explanation of early delinquency and a stable self-control."

This chapter provided the foundation upon which effective interventions can be built.   Only theoretically meaningful and empirically supported interventions will be able to effectively interrupt the deleterious developmental trajectory of serious and violent early offenders.   The next chapter will describe a comprehensive intervention aimed at serious young offenders in a moderately sized Midwestern city.   It will also detail the data, methods, and analytic strategy employed to test its effectiveness at reducing delinquent behavior among that group.

CHAPTER 3

Data, Methods, and Analytic Strategy

This chapter will describe in detail the context of the current study, the specific research questions posed, and the methods by which each question was empirically examined. First, the study context will be presented in terms of a collaborative comprehensive intervention being implemented in a moderately-sized Midwestern city. Second, the sample being studied will be discussed in detail. Third, formal hypotheses will be enumerated which will guide the study. Finally, specific variables and scales to be employed in testing the hypotheses will be described and an analytic strategy will be presented.

STUDY CONTEXT

With technical assistance from the Michigan Justice Statistics Center in the School of Criminal Justice at Michigan State University, police departments in four cities in the Midwest developed and implemented community-based intervention initiatives aimed at serious juvenile offenders between the ages of 10 and 13 years old. Programs in each of the cities began in 2000 and evaluation concluded in 2004. The current analysis focused on data obtained from one of these programs. The particular program at this city was chosen for a number of reasons. First, program administrators adopted and followed clear selection criteria. Specifically, youth between the ages of 10 and 13 who were arrested for the first or second time for a serious offense who lived in a specified area of the city were court-ordered to participate in the program. Second, program administrators at this site worked very closely with the evaluation team to provide comprehensive process and outcome data for the evaluation. Third, the city was the largest among the four sites, and therefore allowed for an adequate sample size for statistical analysis.

The city in which the program was implemented has a population of approximately 200,000 and is the second largest city in the state. Based on the 2000 Census, the city was 49% male, 62% White, 20% African American, and 13% Hispanic or Latino. The city police department employs approximately 387 police officers and about 100 civilian employees. The target area (Westside of the city) was selected by the city police department because it had an increasing crime problem and deteriorating neighborhood conditions. Additionally, residents of this area are generally of lower socioeconomic status than their counterparts in other areas of the city. For example, within the target area, the percent of families with annual income greater than $25,000 is 65.91 compared to 68.45 for the city as a whole. Moreover, the unemployment rate in the target area is 7.6%, compared to 6.1% for the city. Additional demographic characteristics detailing the city and the target area can be found in Table C1 of Appendix C.

Program administrators collaborated with several stakeholders to develop and implement an intense programming model to address the needs of youth who had become involved in delinquent behavior at an early age. The program consisted of three main components. First, all youth who met the eligibility requirements were identified at arrest by the Serious Habitual Offender Team (SHOT) of the city police department. The SHOT team included a number of police officers who had extensive experience working with serious, violent juvenile offenders. Second, all juveniles were fast-tracked by the family court. That is, youth who were identified as fitting the criteria were quickly placed on the caseload of a probation officer participating in the program. The family court was also responsible for completing risk assessments for all youth in the target age group. After being placed on formal probation, each youth was enrolled in the program, which involved intensive supervision probation, including both concentrated surveillance and involvement in pro-social services programming. All probation orders also included mandatory attendance at one of several recreational centers located in the surrounding neighborhood (or other suitable programs as determined by the court). Throughout the program, members of the SHOT and probation teams maintained regular contact with participating youth. A summary of the actions that were taken to change how the youth behaved included continuous surveillance, involvement in recreational activities and life-skills training, and the introduction of positive role models (through mentoring and tutoring programs).

Program administrators at the site detailed the date and nature (e.g., in person or by phone) of contacts by police and probation officers and other program officials. Additional data, including date and duration in minutes, were gathered regarding specific programs in which individuals participated (e.g., counseling, recreation, and community service). Discussions with court administrators and police officers revealed that many of the services incorporated into the intervention had not previously been readily available to this population of offenders. As such, this intervention represented a comprehensive approach to addressing serious delinquent behavior that might otherwise have been overlooked. According to program administrators, prior to this intervention, young offenders were commonly adjusted at intake and released with no formal probation requirements. As a result of this program, therefore, young offenders received services not otherwise available to them.

The intervention was founded on a community policing and probation model that assigned probation officers to supervise a group of offenders who resided in the same general neighborhood. This approach allowed community policing officers and probation officers to coordinate efforts in supervising offenders in the community. Moreover, the juvenile court employed surveillance officers who intensively monitored youth above and beyond traditional probation contacts. Surveillance officers commonly contacted juveniles several times each day (both in person and by phone).

Program administrators noted a number of benefits of the community-based probation model. First, because probation officers were physically located in the neighborhoods, they had better knowledge of the culture of the neighborhood and concerns that residents may have had. Probation officers often attended neighborhood association meetings and residents occasionally stopped by the probation office to discuss issues relating to probation clients. Second, probation officers were able to better understand the needs of the youth and their families because they were able to contact both more regularly. Historically, probation officers typically saw a client once a month; during the current intervention, contacts increased to at least once a week (in addition to the surveillance contacts that occurred daily). Third, probation officers became more aware of services that were available within individual neighborhoods that were of interest to youth and their families. For example, a community organization that is located in the target neighborhood houses a Weed and Seed program and provided youth with recreational programming opportunities.

As described above, many youth involved in the program were court ordered to attend one of several recreational centers in the target neighborhoods. Funding was directed to these centers so that they could provide a safe and secure environment where youth could participate in prosocial activities with peers under the supervision of trained mentors. The largest and most popular of the recreation facilities had a community policing officer assigned to it while open to the youth. Facilities offered various activities including pool, foosball, video games, and organized recreational activities such as basketball. Additionally, all facilities were equipped with computers that were available for youth to work on homework or play various games. Finally, each recreation center organized regular programs such as cooking classes, nature hikes, runs, and other group activities.

All youth involved in the intervention program were subject to intensive supervision and were required to participate in recreational activities. In addition to these standard activities, probation officers ordered specific programming to individuals who had exhibited special programmatic needs. For example, youth who exhibited substance abuse problems were regularly tested for drug or alcohol use and repeat offenders were court ordered to attend drug counseling. Others attended individual psychological counseling, family counseling, or anger management classes. Additionally, the court developed an after-school tutoring program, organized summer recreation camps, and coordinated community service activities for youth to complete within their own neighborhood. In a minority of cases youth were ordered to short-term residential treatment or boot camp for violations of the conditions of probation. As can be seen, the program incorporated common elements yet individualized the program to account for specific needs. According to program administrators, the intervention aimed to instill positive attitudes in youth and to create a positive environment for youth to participate in prosocial activities.

While the family domain was not a primary target of the intervention, some youth participated in family counseling. More specifically, the family counseling employed as an element of this program involved regular sessions (usually weekly or twice a month) with parent(s) and their child or just the youth's parent(s). Therapists all had master's degrees in social work, and were usually employed through the statewide department responsible for youth and family-related issues.

A key aspect of the program was that it addressed the behavior of youth within their familial and neighborhood contexts. While extreme family dysfunction or continued antisocial behavior resulted in an out-of-home placement (detention or foster care), the intervention was based on a community model that kept youth in their homes when possible.

SAMPLE

All of the youth who participated in the intervention were included in the analysis as the treatment group. In addition, a comparison group of officially nondelinquent youth who resided in the same target area was also identified. Comparison group youth were invited to participate in one of two ways. First, they were recruited from the middle school in the target area. Teachers informed youth in their classes about the project, and interested students were required to have their parent or guardian sign and return a permission slip to participate. Because of this active consent procedure, the participation rate was relatively low (about 25%). Second, youth were recruited from two recreation centers in the neighborhood. These were the same recreation centers that many intervention participants were court ordered to attend. Flyers were distributed, and the supervisors at each center agreed to solicit participants. Active consent was also secured from the parents of these youth. All youth (both treatment and comparison) were given $20 for a 30- to 40-minute interview.

Data for this study were collected from program participants and the comparison group of officially nondelinquent offenders using in-person structured interviews (see Appendix A for the questionnaire used) and from official sources (police and school data). Program participants self-reported attitudes, beliefs, behaviors, and relationships with others at three time periods: upon beginning the intervention, approximately 6 months following the initial interview, and approximately 12 months following the initial interview. The current analysis uses data from the first two interviews. Data were collected from comparison youth at two time points, also with approximately 6 months between collection points.

While exceptions exist (e.g., Gottfredson & Hirschi, 1987), the criminological community largely agrees that longitudinal designs are preferable to cross-sectional designs. For example, Farrington (1986:212) reports that one "...advantage of a longitudinal study is its superiority over cross-sectional research in establishing cause and effect, by showing that changes in one factor are followed by changes in another." For this reason, outcome variables (delinquency) were measured at interview 2, while predictor variables were measured at interview 1. In this way, temporal ordering was specified such that cause preceded effect.

Even though the sample does not consist of youth who were randomly selected from a larger population, it builds on traditional school-only samples, which may fail to capture the most active offenders who may be missing due to absence. By recruiting youth from recreational centers and including those who have been arrested, the sample attempts to include the most active and at-risk youth in the target neighborhoods. Indeed, many nationally representative samples of youth may fail to include sufficient numbers of active offenders to allow for accurate analysis (Blumstein et al., 1986; Sampson & Laub, 1993).

Serious juvenile offenders between the ages of 10 and 13 years were targeted for this intervention. Initially, serious nonviolent delinquent offenders were the population of interest. It quickly became apparent (and will be demonstrated in the next chapter) that program administrators also included many violent offenders (youth arrested for criminal sexual conduct or assault). As such, the sample represents youth who were between the ages of 10 and 13 years old when arrested for a serious offense. As discussed in Chapter One, serious offenses include type I index offenses: homicide, rape, robbery, aggravated assault, burglary, theft over $100, motor vehicle theft, and arson. From a research standpoint, this strategy selects individuals who are most likely to be involved in a number of delinquent behaviors. While this approach will yield valuable information about the frequency, intensity, and variety of incidents in which known offenders are involved, and is likely the best way to explain variations in offending, it too has some limitations. The primary limitation concerns external validity. Adolescents who have been adjudicated delinquent are likely to be very different from the broader population of active offenders. These youth may engage in more serious offenses, may be involved in a wider variety of offenses, or may have different social histories than those who are not formally adjudicated delinquent (Loeber & Farrington, 1998). Due to the filtering function of the juvenile justice process, many less-serious offenders are often diverted from the official system and therefore would not be included in a sample of adjudicated delinquents. Focusing on arrestees addresses this latter issue, but some who are arrested may not have actually broken the law. As a result, findings from this study are generalizable only to juveniles between the ages of 10 and 13 who are arrested for a serious (violent or nonviolent) offense.

Table 1 presents the arrest offenses for youth involved in the intervention. As noted, many of the treatment youth had committed a serious personal offense that resulted in their placement into the program. Specifically, approximately 22% committed assault, almost 20% engaged in criminal sexual conduct, and 3% robbed another individual. While the majority of youth were referred to the program for committing a property offense (see Table 2), most were of a serious nature (e.g., home invasion or burglary). Also, even though a few drug and status offenders participated in programming (less than 5%), they did not represent a sizeable segment to the degree that resources were unduly used up by minor offenders. These initial findings suggest that, in general, integrity was maintained in terms of the seriousness of the behaviors committed by program youth.

Table 1. Qualifying Offense Information (83 youth*)

	Percent
B & E/Burglary/Home Invasion	28.9
Assault	21.7
Criminal Sexual Conduct	19.3
Larceny	6.0
Receiving and concealing stolen property	4.8
Retail Fraud	4.8
Auto Theft	3.6
Status (curfew, truancy, runaway)	3.6
Malicious Destruction of Property	2.4
Robbery	2.4
Arson	1.2
Drug and Alcohol	1.2
Total	100.0

*Qualifying offense data were not available for 3 youth.

Table 2. Type of Qualifying Offense (83 youth)

	Percent
Property	51.8
Personal	43.4
Status	3.6
Drug	1.2
Total	100.0

Sampson and Laub (1993) note that most large-scale longitudinal studies of adolescent development fail to sample sufficient numbers of serious and/or persistent offenders (see also Blumstein et al., 1986). While the sample employed here was not large, it is comprised entirely of youth who have exhibited serious behavioral problems. Similarly, Moffitt (1993) argues that criminological research using adolescent samples may be inherently flawed because it commonly equates to comparing "apples and oranges;" that is, the grouping of serious and nonserious offenders (see also, Mullis, et al., 2005). This study avoids this criticism by focusing only on pre-adolescent offenders; those Moffitt (1993) would characterize as at an elevated risk to become life-course persistent offenders. Because the subjects initiated offending in childhood and engaged in serious delinquent behaviors, they represent some of the most at-risk for continuing to engage in deviance throughout the life course.

Sample Attrition

Many of the youth who participated in the program moved several times or were otherwise difficult to locate for follow-up interviews. There is a sizeable population of migrant workers in the target area, and, as a result, several families moved considerable distance away from the city, including some even leaving the country. With assistance from program administrators, the research team made numerous attempts to contact missing individuals, but was often unsuccessful. Attrition is a common problem in longitudinal research designs as participants become difficult to track down for follow-up interviews (Menard, 1991). Specific biases may taint results if youth who were re-interviewed differ significantly from those who were not re-interviewed. For example, follow-up interviews that missed the most delinquent of youth may misrepresent differences that emerge at the second interview. To determine the extent to which attrition may negatively influence the results of this study, descriptive statistics were calculated for youth for which two interviews were obtained and compared to youth who were only interviewed at one time point.

In total, 68 out of the 86 treatment youth (79.1%) and 83 out of the original 135 comparison youth (61.5%) participated in a follow-up interview. Table 3 notes some differences between those who were successfully re-interviewed for this study and those who were not. Among the treatment group males and younger youth were more likely to receive a follow-up interview. Among the comparison group, female and white youth were more likely to participate in the second interview. Moreover, in the comparison group youth who received a follow-up interview reported a stronger bond to their primary caretaker and were generally less delinquent at the first interview. This finding is problematic, but not entirely unexpected. Because participation was completely voluntary for the comparison group (and only slightly more encouraged for the treatment group) it is not surprising that youth involved in delinquent behavior were less likely to submit to be interviewed a second time. Even though participants were reassured that study staff were not associated with school, police, or other formal social control agencies, and confidentiality was repeatedly stressed, some youth may have not felt comfortable continuing to participate. This problem is not unique to the current study, and likely permeates many repeated-measure designs. Nevertheless, based on these attrition diagnostics, results should be interpreted accordingly.

Missing values are not otherwise problematic with these data. If values were missing, however, the cases were excluded listwise for all analyses. The final sample consists of 68 treatment youth and 83 comparison youth who were interviewed at least two times over the course of six to nine months.

HYPOTHESES

All of the following hypotheses sought to assess the importance of family relationships on intervention success for young offenders. As reviewed above, the family is especially important among young individuals (pre-adolescent or younger). As such, this study explicitly tested the importance of family relationships on intervention success with this special population of offenders. The first two hypotheses focused on conditions at the beginning of the intervention, while the latter two hypotheses tested the effect of intervention-influenced changes in family relationships.

Table 3. Attrition Diagnostics

	Treatment Group			Comparison Group		
	i1	i2	missing	i1	i2	missing
Number	86	68	18 (20.9%)	135	83	52 (38.5%)
% Male	80.0	94.0	76.0*	57.0	49.0	69.0*
% White	50.0	45.6	66.7	34.1	41.0	23.1*
Mean Age	12.4	12.2	13.0*	11.9	11.9	11.9
Mean Family Bond	3.30	3.29	3.36	3.53	3.59	3.43*
% Single Parent	74.4	75.0	72.2	39.3	37.3	42.3
i1 SR Violent	75.6	77.9	66.7	45.9	38.6	57.7*
i1 SR Nonviolent	72.1	69.1	83.3	35.6	31.3	42.3
i1 SR Drug	66.2	67.7	61.1	16.3	10.8	25.0*

Significant difference between missing and i2 - p* < .05 (two-tailed test)

64

The primary research question for this study was: *What role do family relationships play in predicting intervention success among serious childhood offenders?* Additionally, are early serious offenders are more amenable to treatment efforts if they begin the intervention having strong relationships with their parent(s)? Specifically, the first hypothesis asserted:

Hypothesis 1. Youth who have a strong relationship with their primary caretaker upon beginning an intervention are more likely to abstain from offending.

Based on the theoretical and empirical evidence reviewed above, it was hypothesized that youth who reported a strong family bond at the start of the intervention were more likely to desist. As discussed in Chapter 1, a wealth of information exists that predicts that youth who have a strong prosocial relationship with a parent are less likely to become involved in deviant or delinquent behavior. The question remains whether strong relationships with parents also help youth in an intervention context.

Strong relationships with parents provide youth with a supportive environment within which delinquency desistance could occur. A youth who is strongly attached to his or her parent is more likely to trust in his or her advice and follow directives given by that parent. Strong communication indicates that the child is willing to discuss problems with his or her parent. Sufficient supervision suggests that parents know what their children are doing, and therefore are able to control deviant behavior and reinforce prosocial decision-making. Finally, parents who employ creative and positive parenting skills are better able to manage stressful situations. As detailed below, the measure of family bond employed in the current analysis included elements of all of these family dynamics (attachment, communication, supervision, and parenting skills).

The second hypothesis examined the effects of family structure at intake on intervention success:

Hypothesis 2.   Youth living with two parents upon beginning the intervention are more likely to abstain from offending.

As reviewed in Chapter 1, a growing body of research suggests that youth living in a single-parent family are at an elevated risk for delinquency, drug use, and other undesirable outcomes. Two parents can more effectively supervise their children, which may buffer them from other negative pressures, such as the influence of deviant peers. On the other hand, others have noted that it is not the structure of the family that is important, but the quality of the relationship between parent and child (Van Voorhis, Cullen, Mathers, & Garner, 1988). While the first hypothesis addressed the importance of quality, this hypothesis considers structure.

The third hypothesis assessed the importance of including family programming (such as family counseling) in interventions that target young offenders.

Hypothesis 3.   Youth who received family-focused programming are more likely to abstain from offending.

While many of the youth did not receive family-based programming, it is hypothesized that those who did will be more likely to desist. Family-based programs have demonstrated more effectiveness at rehabilitating juvenile offenders than programs that do not target the family domain (Latimer, 2001; Perkins-Dock, 2001). Moreover, when included as one of many programmatic activities for youth, family-focused programming may prove especially effective.

The final hypothesis examined the extent to which youth who improved their relationship with their primary caretaker were more successful at abstaining from delinquency during the intervention.

Hypothesis 4.   Youth participating in the intervention who report improved family relations from interview 1 to interview 2 are more likely to abstain from offending.

Even though many individuals began the intervention reporting relatively poor relationships with their primary caretaker, if these relations improved—either as a direct result of the intervention or not—it is hypothesized that behavior will also improve. Some youth participated in family counseling, while others received a variety of other programming that may have indirectly resulted in improvement in the relationship between the child and his or her parent(s). Moreover, all treatment youth were placed on intensive supervision, which required them to be at specified locations throughout the day, including being home by a specified time. These restrictions may have resulted in the youth spending more time at home or with parents thereby possibly improving their family relationship.

ANALYTIC STRATEGY

Dependent Variables

Both official and self-reported measures of delinquent involvement were employed as separate outcome variables in this study. It is important to note that official and self-reported measures of delinquent behavior are independent approximations of one's actual involvement in delinquent behavior (Thornberry & Krohn, 2000). Moreover, researchers recognize that both self-report and official measures of delinquency have notable sources of error (Maxfield, Weiler, and Widom, 2000:108). For example, due to inconsistencies in measurement and possible screening biases throughout the justice process, the reliability of official statistics has been questioned for years (Hindelang, Hirschi, & Weis, 1981). Undoubtedly, a significant number of individuals who break the law are not apprehended and therefore are not included in official reports of delinquency. Finally, a wide range of deviant activities that are of interest to juvenile delinquency researchers are often not captured by official reports, such as truancy, parental defiance, or sexual behaviors.

Official recidivism was measured using arrest records of the individual for the six months following the initial interview. This approximates the time that the youth was still involved in the intervention, though some youth may have already been discharged. Individuals who were not rearrested following the first interview were coded a success using a binary variable (0). Any arrest, excluding technical violations of probation, was coded failure (1).

Self-reported involvement in delinquent behavior was measured at the second interview using three unique prevalence scores: violent offending, nonviolent offending, and drug or alcohol use. This strategy more clearly specified the types of behavior in which the juvenile was involved. In contrast, studies which operationalize delinquency as a frequency of a wide variety of offenses may blur the extent to which the individual is involved in serious offending (Loeber et al., 1998). In addition, because a different reference period was used for the first interview (previous 12 months) and the second interview (previous 6 months) in this study, frequency measures of involvement in delinquent behavior that were collected may misrepresent participation in those activities. For example, a youth who reported smoking everyday would be coded as having smoked 365 times at interview 1 and 180 times at interview 2. Even though the youth was still involved in the activity at the same frequency, statistically it would appear that the youth decreased involvement by 50%. While prevalence scores are a conservative estimate of the frequency and intensity of participation in specific activities, the strategy allowed for an understanding of what factors may have contributed to desistance.

The three prevalence scores each included multiple offenses in an effort to measure the extent to which youth were involved in a specified type of offending. Violent offenses included: assaulting a peer, assaulting an adult, and throwing rocks or bottles at other people. Nonviolent offenses included: malicious destruction of property, theft from parents, trespassing, theft from car, shoplifting, graffiti, arson, and auto theft. Drug and alcohol use included: consumed any liquor, smoked marijuana, smoked cigarettes, and used cocaine. Youth who reported at the second interview that they abstained from engaging in violent behaviors since the previous interview were coded as desistors (0) for that offense type. This group of offenders also included youth who did not participate in the activity during the 12 months preceding the initial interview. Individuals who reported any involvement were coded as persistors (1). This group also includes those youth who were initiators—youth who did not engage in those specific behaviors prior to interview 1 but did so (perhaps for the first time) between interviews. This strategy was also employed for nonviolent offending and drug and alcohol use.

Independent Variables

As discussed above, the main independent variable for this analysis is the strength of the relationship a youth has with his or her primary caretaker. Respondents were asked questions about their mother and father (or, if applicable, a different guardian) if they resided with him or her (or both) for the majority of the six months preceding the interview. A primary caretaker variable was created which represented the parent with whom the child reported spending the most time during the assessment period.

The family bond scale consists of items pertaining to the relationship participants had with their primary caretaker (see table 4). Confirmatory factor analysis was employed to ensure that each of the variables measured the same underlying construct (family bond). After confirmation, a mean score was computed for family bond that included the following 10 questions: (1) "I feel I can really trust my primary caretaker;" (2) "I really enjoy my primary caretaker;" (3) "I think my primary caretaker is terrific;" (4) "I feel proud of my primary caretaker;" (5) "I feel I can trust my primary caretaker with just about anything I tell him/her;" (6) "I talk to my primary caretaker about trouble I am having at work or school;" (7) "I go places or do things with my primary caretaker;" (8) "I think highly of my primary caretaker;" (9) "my primary caretaker is a person I want to be like;" and (10) "I really enjoy spending time with my primary caretaker."

The response set for items 1-4 was "never," "once in a while," "sometimes," and "always." For items 5-7, the response set was "very likely," "likely," "unlikely," and "very unlikely." Finally, the response set for items 8-10 was "strongly agree," "agree," "disagree," and "strongly disagree." All items loaded on a single factor with loadings greater than 0.5. Some items were reverse coded such that higher values on the mean scale indicated a stronger relationship with one's parents.[4]

In addition to using a mean score as continuous variables representing the level of bonding a youth has to his or her parent at the first interview, a change score was created representing the change in family bond from interview 1 to interview 2. That is, the mean score at time 2 was subtracted from the mean score at time 1. Positive values represent improvement in family bonding while negative values represent deteriorating family bonding. It was hypothesized that youth who report improved relations with their parents will be more likely to desist offending. To be sure, not all youth will report improvement in family bonding over time. Those who do experience an

---

[4] While some have suggested that problems arise when the number of variables used to comprise a scale approaches N, Marsh & Hau (1999) demonstrate that in most cases, the higher the number of indicators per construct, the more valid and reliable the measure

improvement in family bonding, it is hypothesized, will be more likely to discontinue offending.

Table 4. Family Bond Component Variables and Factor Loadings

	Factor Loading
1. I feel I can really trust my primary caretaker	0.616
2. I really enjoy my primary caretaker	0.776
3. I think my primary caretaker is terrific	0.786
4. I feel proud of my primary caretaker	0.623
5. I feel I can trust my primary caretaker with just about anything	0.752
6. I talk to my primary caretaker about trouble I am having at work or school	0.539
7. I go places or do things with my primary caretaker	0.759
8. I think highly of my primary caretaker	0.616
9. My primary caretaker is a person I want to be like	0.708
10. I really enjoy spending time with my primary caretaker	0.730
Eigenvalue: 4.83	
Cronbach's Alpha: 0.875	

The number of minutes of family-based programming (generally family counseling) was also used to predict intervention success. As noted, it was hypothesized that youth who received family-based programming such as family counseling would be more likely to desist offending. These data were obtained from program administrators who documented the dates and duration (in minutes) of all programs in which the intervention youth participated. Finally, family structure was operationalized as single-parent (coded "1") and two-parent (coded "0") households.

Control Variables

Because a small sample was used for this study (86 treatment and 135 comparison youth), few additional variables can be added to the models while maintaining sufficient statistical power. This is particularly true for the longitudinal analyses in which the sample size was even smaller (68 treatment and 83 comparison youth). Thus, only four control variables were added to the multivariate models. Age (age in years), ethnicity (white/nonwhite), and gender (male/female) were used to control for the individual effects of each of these variables. Additionally, for the treatment group, the number of days between the intake date and the initial interview was included as a control for any treatment received prior to the initial interview. Even though the research team attempted to interview treatment youth immediately upon beginning the program, delays inevitably occurred.

Quantitative Models and Methods

In the first stage of this analysis, data are presented to describe the sample being studied. Relatively few existing studies have focused on young serious offenders; therefore, information gleaned from these initial analyses will provide researchers and practitioners with a better understanding of the characteristics unique to this population. Specifically, descriptive statistics were conducted for all of the variables being employed in later analyses. Group means were compared using independent samples t-tests to determine if there were any statistically significant differences between the comparison and delinquent groups on important characteristics (including self-reported delinquency and family bond).

The next stage of this analysis involved statistical analyses to test each of the hypotheses enumerated above. Where appropriate, models were estimated for both the treatment and comparison groups, so that any differences between the groups could be ascertained. Conducting a combined analysis with both groups would not allow for the comparison of changes over time (the comparison of slopes). It is already known that the two groups differ in terms of their family relationships at the time of the first interview. This study seeks to determine whether there are significant differences between the two groups in terms of how participants change over time. If delinquent youth improve their relationship with their parent(s) more dramatically than the comparison youth, some of those changes may be attributable to the intervention (although lack of random assignment to each group precludes any degree of certainty).

Bivariate and multivariate logistic regression analysis was performed to assess the impact of continuous predictor variables (strength of family bond, change in family bond, and family programming received) on each of the binary outcome variables (self reported violent, nonviolent, and drug offending, and official delinquency). The final multivariate models examined the extent to which familial relationships and family programming were important while controlling for the effects of age, ethnicity, gender, and previous treatment. Contingency table analysis was used to determine the relationship between family structure at interview 1 and future delinquency.

The final stage of the analysis employed Hierarchical Linear Modeling (HLM) to further test the association between the strength of the family bond at interview 1 and future delinquency (Raudenbush, Bryk, Cheong, & Congdon, 2000). There are a number of advantages to using HLM. First, modeling change within the individual using HLM does not require that the spacing be the same between observations (Raudenbush & Bryk, 2002). Additionally, HLM also considers the effect of individuals for whom a subsequent interview was not obtained (Raudenbush & Bryk, 2002). Finally, HLM allows for the use of parallel scores to represent the measurement of key concepts, which estimates statistical models for a (albeit artificially) larger sample. Specifically, as discussed above, the family bond concept in the current study was measured using ten variables that estimate the relationship youth have with his or her primary caretaker. Parallel scores were created by computing two mean scores that each used five of the variables from the original operationalization of family bond. Variables can be assigned randomly (see, Lyons, Zarit, Sayer, & Whitlatch, 2002) or deliberately to ensure similar variances (Coley & Morris, 2002). The latter method was chosen for the current study. Theoretically, the two scores still represent a latent approximation of the relationship each youth has with his or her primary caretaker.

Assumptions and Diagnostics

The primary quantitative method employed in the current study was logistic regression. Logistic regression is the variation of regression most appropriate for models that include a dichotomous outcome variable. Using a maximum-likelihood estimation method, logistic regression predicts the odds (or likelihood) of an event occurring given specified conditions (or independent variables). While logistic regression is not constrained by all of the assumptions of ordinary least squares (OLS) regression (Menard, 1995), there are some assumptions that need to be kept in mind. For example, both OLS and logistic regression assume that the model is correctly specified. Including irrelevant or excluding relevant variables can result in a misspecified model. This is less a concern for the proposed study because the purpose of this research is not to test the merits of a particular theory per se, but to assess the predictive power of one construct common in many theories (family bond) on an outcome variable. Statistically, the odds ratio [Exp(B)] will be of more interest in this study than the explained variance (r^2). Nevertheless, there could be additional variables not considered that may affect the way a person's family bond influences delinquency.

Collinearity is another potential problem that can negatively bias both OLS and logistic regression models (Menard, 1995).

Independent variables that are highly correlated may result in inflated standard errors, thereby increasing the likelihood of Type II error. Collinearity was initially assessed by reviewing the bivariate correlations between all variables (see Tables B1 and B2, in Appendix B). No predictor variables included in any of the models together were significantly related to each other. Collinearity statistics were also computed in OLS to determine the influence of relationships between independent variables. Specifically, tolerance statistics below 0.20 (Menard, 1995) and variance inflation factors greater than 1.5 (Fox, 1991) may indicate a problem. With regard to multicollinearity, variance inflation factors (VIF) ranged between 1.012 and 1.087 and tolerance statistics ranged between 0.920 and 0.988 which suggests little cause for concern (Fox, 1991).

Unlike OLS, logistic regression does not assume that errors are normally distributed or homoscedastic (Menard, 1995). As such, influential outliers are not as problematic using logistic regression. As a final diagnostic, however, standardized residuals were computed and Cook's Distance (D) statistic was reviewed with an eye toward values inconsistent with others. Cases with extreme residuals do not fit the model and therefore may indicate a typology that is inconsistent with the current hypotheses. Standardized residuals ranged from -1.808 to 1.296 and Cook's D ranged from 0.000 to 0.075. These numbers are not indicative of problematic cases in the sample.

SUMMARY

For a number of reasons, the current research represents an important contribution to the criminological literature. First, few studies have focused on serious juvenile delinquents between the ages of 10 and 13. As discussed above, youth who initiate offending at this early age are at a greater risk to become career criminals. Successfully interrupting their paths at an early age can result in substantial fiscal as well as social benefits. Second, this study attempts to demonstrate that the influence of the family is an important dimension often missing from juvenile interventions. Results from this study will help program developers in creating interventions that are responsive to the needs of serious juvenile offenders. It also demonstrates how a common element from several criminological theories (family influences) can be used to ground intervention efforts. The following chapter presents the results of several statistical tests conducted to test the four hypotheses presented.

CHAPTER 4
Findings

As should be clear by now, the purpose of this study was to assess the importance of targeting family relationships in interventions aimed at young offenders. Another notable characteristic of this research was that hypotheses were tested using a unique sample, namely, *serious* young offenders. In testing the hypotheses enumerated in Chapter 3, this chapter will proceed in the following stages. First, sample characteristics will be presented, followed by a comparative look at the differences between the delinquent group and a comparison group. Second, each of the hypotheses will be tested, in turn, using both bivariate and multivariate statistical models estimated for both the treatment and comparison groups in an effort to ascertain any differences between the groups in terms of the influence of the family on future delinquency. Because very few youth in the comparison group were arrested in the 6 months following the initial interview as gleaned from official reports (less than 4%), statistical models for these youth will rely on self-reported outcome measures. Finally, Hierarchical Linear Modeling was employed to conduct additional analyses aimed at better understanding the relationship between familial relationships and delinquent behavior in an intervention context. Taken together, these methods seek to illuminate the association between family characteristics and future delinquent behaviors.

DESCRIPTIVE STATISTICS

As reported in Table 5, 80% of the treatment youth were male, 50% were white, 24% were African American, and 24% were Hispanic or Mexican. As specified by the program model, the vast majority of youth (87.2%) were between 10 and 13 years old when first interviewed (mean=12.4). Finally, most of the treatment youth (75.6%) were in junior high school (grades 6-8) while participating in the program. There are some notable differences between the intervention and comparison groups. For example, 43% of comparison youth were female, 34% were white, 31% were Hispanic or Mexican, and 27% were African American. Moreover, the treatment group was older and more advanced in schooling than the comparison group. Due to these differences, results based on comparisons of the two groups must be interpreted with caution.

Table 6 presents statistics describing the nature of the family environment for both the treatment and comparison groups. For example, 74% of treatment youth and 39% of the comparison youth lived with one parent at the time of the first interview. Moreover, as predicted by the theories reviewed in Chapter 2, treatment (officially delinquent) youth reported a weaker bond with their primary caretaker than comparison (officially nondelinquent) youth. Over time, the average family bond decreased for both groups at about the same rate. This trend is consistent with developmental research which indicates that during adolescence youth move away from the family and toward the peer group as a primary influence (Warr, 2002). This finding also initially indicates that the intervention did little to improve family relationships among the treatment youth as a whole. Because the current study lacks a control group of delinquent youth who did not receive intervention programming, it is uncertain whether the family relationships of delinquent youth would have deteriorated further without the programming.

Table 5. Descriptive Characteristics of the Treatment and Comparison Groups

	Treatment (N=86)		Comparison (N=135)		Total (N = 221)	
	N	*Percent*	*N*	*Percent*	*N*	*Percent*
Male	69	80.2	77	57.0	146	66.1
Female	17	19.8	58	43.0	75	33.9
Race						
African American	21	24.4	37	27.4	58	26.2
Hispanic/ Mexican	21	24.4	42	31.1	63	28.5
White	43	50.0	46	34.1	89	40.3
Native American	1	1.2	0	0.0	1	0.5
Biracial	0	0.0	6	4.4	6	2.7
Missing	0	0.0	4	3.0	4	1.8
Age						
9	3	3.5	4	3.0	7	3.2
10	4	4.7	16	11.9	20	9.0
11	9	10.5	37	20.0	46	20.8
12	21	24.4	38	28.1	59	26.7
13	41	47.7	43	31.9	84	38.0
14	8	9.3	4	3.0	12	5.4
15	0	0.0	2	1.5	2	0.9
Mean	12.36		11.90*			
(Std. Dev.)	(1.16)		(1.23)			
Grade						
3	2	2.3	1	0.7	3	1.4
4	3	3.5	16	11.9	19	8.6
5	5	5.8	12	8.9	17	7.7
6	17	19.8	30	22.2	47	21.3
7	26	30.2	39	28.9	65	29.4
8	22	25.6	17	12.6	39	17.6
9	5	5.8	0	0.0	5	2.3
Missing	6	7.0	20	14.8	26	11.8
Mean	6.85		6.23*			
(Std. Dev.)	(1.31)		(1.28)			

*Mean difference $p < .05$ (two-tailed test).

Table 6. Family Relationships by Group

	Treatment (N=68)		Comparison (N=83)	
	Mean	*Std. Dev.*	*Mean*	*Std. Dev.*
Single Parent Family	0.74	0.44	0.37*	0.49
Family Bond				
Interview 1	3.29	0.56	3.59*	0.39
Interview 2	3.27	0.54	3.57*	0.42
Change over time	-0.016	0.54	-0.018	0.33
Family Programming[1]	379.14	257.31	--	--

[1]Mean number of minutes of family programming for youth who received it.
*Mean difference statistically significant (p < .05; two-tailed test).

Table 7 displays the self-reported and official delinquency of all youth. Almost 78% of treatment youth and 39% of comparison youth reported participation in violent behaviors in the 12 months preceding the initial interview. Significantly fewer youth in both groups reported participation in these behaviors in the 6 months leading up to the second interview; about 63% of treatment youth and less than 22% of comparison youth reported violent behaviors at interview 2. There was also a substantial (though not statistically significant) decrease in the percent of youth reporting involvement in nonviolent delinquency. The percentage of treatment youth involved in nonviolent offending dropped from 69 to 56, while comparison youth involved in the same behaviors decreased from 31% to less than 22%. Moreover, fewer youth in both groups reported using drugs or alcohol (67.6% to 51.5% for treatment youth and 10.8% to 8.4% for comparison youth). Finally, about 22% of treatment youth were arrested in the six months following the initial interview compared to less than 4% of the comparison youth.

Findings from the first stage of analysis indicate that there are some important differences between the comparison and treatment groups in terms of demographic characteristics, family structure and bond, and self-reported delinquency. Notably, the treatment youth start out with a weaker bond to their primary caretaker than their comparison counterparts, but this relationship changed over time at about an equal rate for both groups. This finding suggests that the intervention was not successful at improving family relationships among treatment youth. Additionally, fewer youth from both groups reported participating in delinquent behavior and drug use at the second interview. Decreases were more dramatic for the treatment youth, suggesting the improvement may have been associated with intervention programming. The following sections will, in turn, evaluate the empirical support for the four hypotheses outlined in Chapter 3.

Table 7. Self-Reported and Official Offending Characteristics

	Treatment (N=68)		Comparison (N=83)	
	Number	*Percent*	*Number*	*Percent*
Interview 1				
Self-reported violent	53	77.9	32	38.6
Self-reported nonviolent	47	69.1	26	31.3
Self-reported drug use	46	67.6	9	10.8
Interview 2				
Self-reported violent	43	63.2*	18	21.7*
Self-reported nonviolent	38	55.9	18	21.7
Self-reported drug use	35	51.5*	7	8.4
6 month official failure	15	22.1	5	3.7

*Represents a statistically significant difference from interview 1 (p < .05; two-tailed test)

HYPOTHESIS 1: FAMILY BOND AT INTAKE AND DELINQUENCY DESISTANCE

The first question this study addressed was upon beginning an intervention what effect do family relationships have intervention success? Simply put, do youth who begin an intervention with a strong bond to their parent(s) succeed at desisting offending at a disproportionate rate compared to youth who are not strongly bonded to their parent(s)? Using logistic regression analysis, this stage of the study modeled the association between the strength of the family bond at intake (interview 1) and future delinquency (interview 2).

As specified in Hypothesis 1, it is expected that youth with a strong bond to their primary caretaker will be more likely to desist offending. Tables 8 through 11 display results from the logistic regression analysis. While most relationships did not achieve statistical significance, a negative association between family bond and delinquency emerged in almost all of the bivariate and multivariate models. For the treatment group, the stronger the family bond at intake into the program, the less likely the youth was to self-report future participation in violent activities and drug use. A small and insignificant positive relationship emerged between strength of family bond and future self-reported nonviolent behaviors. In terms of control variables, age was positively related to delinquency; that is, older youth were more likely to report involvement in delinquency and to be arrested.

Among members of the treatment group, number of days of programming prior to the first interview was inconsistently related to delinquency. Youth who were in the program longer prior to being interviewed for the first time were more likely to self-report drug use and to be rearrested (statistically significant); however, these youth were less likely to self-report violent or nonviolent offending (not statistically significant). These findings are difficult to explain, and require additional analysis to better understand. One possibility is that the nature and quality of the programming in the early days may have varied and youth may not have had the opportunity to learn from the programming to the extent that changes in their behavior would be evident.

Similar findings emerged for the comparison youth. For example, though not statistically significant, youth who reported a strong bond with their primary caretaker were generally less likely to self-report future delinquent behavior. Among both groups, males and older youth were generally more likely to self-report involvement in delinquency and drug use.

Table 8. Bivariate Logistic Regression – Family Bond at Intake (Treatment Group)

	Official Delinquency		Self-Reported Violent		Self-Reported Nonviolent		Self-Reported Drug Use	
	Coeff.	Exp(B)	Coeff.	Exp(B)	Coeff.	Exp(B)	Coeff.	Exp(B)
Constant	-.580 (1.530)		.865 (1.528)		.001 1.463		.793 (1.472)	
Family Bond at Intake	-.187 (.461)	.830	-.098 (.457)	.907	.072 (.349)	1.074	-.223 (.441)	.800
Cox & Snell R^2	.002		.001		.000		.004	
Nagelkerke R^2	.003		.001		.001		.005	

Note: standard errors in parentheses; N=68 (except in official delinquency model, N=86)

Table 9. Multivariate Logistic Regression – Family Bond at Intake (Treatment Group)

	Official Delinquency		Self-Reported Violent		Self-Reported Nonviolent		Self-Reported Drug Use	
	Coeff.	Exp(B)	Coeff.	Exp(B)	Coeff.	Exp(B)	Coeff.	Exp(B)
Constant	-9.772*		-.794		-1.470		-9.173	
	(4.438)		(3.152)		(2.994)		(3.794)	
White	-.632	.532	-.632	.532	-.030	.971	.339	1.404
	(.557)		(.531)		(.501)		(.563)	
Male	-.315	.730	.556	1.744	.684	1.982	.292	1.340
	(-.704)		(.626)		(.589)		(.661)	
Age	.727*	2.070	.216	1.241	.106	1.111	.662*	1.939
	(.327)		(.215)		(.206)		(.260)	
Days in Program	.006*	1.006	-.004	.996	-.001	.999	.011**	1.011
	(.003)		(.003)		(.003)		(.004)	
Family Bond at Intake	-.245	.783	-.279	.757	.010	1.010	-.089	.915
	(.534)		(.493)		(.449)		(.503)	
Cox & Snell R^2	.133		.090		.026		.215	
Nagelkerke R^2	.200		.123		.035		.286	

Note: standard errors in parentheses; N=68 (except in official delinquency model, N=86); *p < .05; **p < .05 (two-tailed test)

Table 10. Bivariate Logistic Regression – Family Bond at Interview 1 (Comparison Group; N=83)

	Self-Reported Violent		Self-Reported Nonviolent		Self-Reported Drug Use	
	Coeff.	Exp(B)	Coeff.	Exp(B)	Coeff.	Exp(B)
Constant	2.259		4.075		-.334	
	(2.277)		(2.389)		(3.147)	
Family Bond at Interview 1	-.997	.369	-1.515*	.220	-.577	.562
	(.642)		(.678)		(.889)	
Cox & Snell R^2	.028		.063		.005	
Nagelkerke R^2	.044		.097		.011	

Note: standard errors in parentheses; *$p < .05$ (two-tailed test)

Table 11. Multivariate Logistic Regression – Family Bond at Interview 1 (Comparison Group; N=83)

	Self-Reported Violent		Self-Reported Nonviolent		Self-Reported Drug Use	
	Coeff.	Exp(B)	Coeff.	Exp(B)	Coeff.	Exp(B)
Constant	-.920		4.434		14.049*	
	(4.014)		(4.677)		(6.700)	
White	.846	2.331	1.291	3.635	1.322	3.749
	(.657)		(.694)		(1.013)	
Male	.920	2.508	-.406	.666	2.604*	13.517
	(.626)		(.641)		(1.231)	
Age	.177	1.193	.096	1.100	.811*	2.251
	(.231)		(.252)		(.389)	
Family Bond at Interview 1	-.945	.389	-2.059*	.128	-.225	.799
	(.676)		(.862)		(1.072)	
Cox & Snell R^2	.076		.136		.153	
Nagelkerke R^2	.118		.210		.348	

Note: standard errors in parentheses; *$p < .05$ (two-tailed test)

In short, while there appears to be a negative relationship between strength of family bond at interview 1 and later delinquency, differences observed were inconsistent and often failed to achieve statistical significance. Moreover, because results were relatively similar for both the treatment and comparison groups, it does not appear that the intervention improved the delinquency-prevention capabilities of a strong bond with a parent. This finding is contrary to what was hypothesized.

HYPOTHESIS 2: FAMILY STRUCTURE AT INTAKE AND DELINQUENCY DESISTANCE

Table 12 presents results from a contingency table analysis testing the relationship between family structure at intake and delinquency for the treatment youth. The chi-square coefficient was employed to test the null hypothesis that there is no relationship between family structure and delinquency. Because the chi-square statistic was not statistically significant in any of the models, there does not appear to be a relationship between family structure and delinquency – contrary to hypothesis 2. Moreover, a higher proportion of youth who lived with two parents persisted in delinquent activity than those who lived with only one parent (except for the drug use model). In short, results indicate no relationship between family structure and delinquency desistance in the treatment sample.

Table 13 presents the findings from the same contingency table analysis (family structure and delinquency) for the comparison group. Again, there does not appear to be a significant relationship between family structure at interview 1 and self-reported delinquency at interview 2. In two of the models (violent and nonviolent offending), youth living with only one parent were more likely to be involved in offending, however, this relationship did not hold for the drug and alcohol use model.

Table 12. Contingency Table Analysis: Family Structure at Intake and Future Delinquency (Treatment Group; N=68)

		6 Month Official Delinquency	Self-Reported Violent[1]	Self-Reported Non-violent[1]	Self-Reported Drug Use[1]
Single-Parent	NO (N=17)	29.4	70.6	64.7	47.1
	YES (N=51)	19.6	60.8	52.9	52.9
Chi-square		.399	.468	.398	.674
Phi		-.102	-.088	-.103	.051

Values represent percent delinquent in each category
[1]Reported delinquency at interview 2

Table 13. Contingency Table Analysis: Family Structure at Intake and Future Delinquency (Comparison Group; N=83)

		Self-Reported Violent[1]	Self-Reported Nonviolent[1]	Self-Reported Drug Use[1]
Single-Parent	NO (N=52)	21.2	19.2	9.6
	YES (N=31)	22.6	25.8	6.5
Chi-square		.879	.482	.616
Phi		.017	.077	-.055

Values represent percentage delinquent in each category
[1]Reported delinquency at interview 2.

Taken together, results are largely equivocal, and do not allow for a better understanding of the relationship between family structure and delinquency, regardless of whether or not a child was involved in intervention programming. Better specification of the type of family structure may be necessary. For example, youth who live in a two-parent household in which one of the parents is a non-biological guardian (step-parent) may be more at risk for participation in delinquency (Demuth & Brown, 2004). Moreover, youth who reside with two deviant parents may be more at risk than youth who live with one prosocial parent. Finally, previous research has identified differential effects with the loss of the mother versus loss of the father (Hass et al., 2004). These issues suggest that a simple dichotomy between one- and two-parent households may be inadequate in assessing risk. Type of relationship (or strength of affect), however, may be a more important characteristic of family dynamics.

HYPOTHESIS 3: FAMILY BASED PROGRAMMING AND DELINQUENCY DESISTANCE

Hypothesis 3 seeks to better understand the effect of family programming on delinquency among members of the treatment group. Because many effective interventions focus on improving family functioning (e.g., Functional Family Therapy, Parent Management Training), it was hypothesized that youth who received family based programming would be more likely to desist. Using logistic regression, this hypothesis was tested by determining the relationship between total number of minutes of family programming received and future delinquency. Tables 14 and 15 report the results of this analysis. Both at the bivariate and multivariate level, odds ratios were very close to 1.0 (0.998-1.002), indicating that the family programming in the current intervention had little effect on either self-reported or official delinquency. Consistent with previous analyses, age and number of days in the program were positively related to drug use and official delinquency.

Table 16 presents the distribution of persistent offenders by treatment received (comparison group who received no treatment, basic treatment group who received intensive supervision and participated in recreational and other general programming, and a family treatment group who received the same programming as the basic treatment group but who also participated in family counseling). Matched pair t-tests were used to assess the significance of changes in the percent of youth self-reporting delinquency over time. As noted in Table 16, the proportion of comparison youth reporting all forms of deviant behavior decreased over time (the only significant difference was in the percent reporting violent offending). Specifically, about 39% of comparison youth reported violent offending at interview 1, compared to less than 22% reporting the same behaviors at interview 2. Similar decreases were noted for nonviolent offending (from 31.3% to 21.7%) and drug use (from 10.8% to 8.4%). It is unclear what mechanism caused these changes; it could be that more delinquent youth in the comparison group were unavailable for the follow-up interview (see attrition analysis in Chapter 3) or that the shorter follow-up period (6 months compared to 12 months) did not allow ample time for participation in these activities.

Encouraging findings emerged for the basic treatment group in that significantly fewer youth reported all forms of offending. For example, almost 87% of the basic treatment youth reported violent offending at interview 1 compared to about 62% at interview 2. Equally dramatic was the decrease in the percent of youth in the basic treatment group who reported involvement in nonviolent offending (from 78.4% to 48.7%) and drug use (from 75.7% to 54.1%). These findings are promising for the intervention as a whole in that they suggest modest short-term improvement in the behavior of the basic treatment group.

The crux of the current study and hypothesis 3, however, is to assess the importance of family treatment among serious young offenders. The third group (family treatment group) received the same general services as the basic treatment group, but also participated in some form of family counseling. Data presented in the last three columns of Table 16 suggest that these youth did not respond as well to the intervention as the basic treatment group did. No statistically significant decreases were reported for any form of offending. In fact the percent of youth involved in nonviolent offending increased.

While it is difficult to explain the failure of family programming to emerge as an important component in this intervention program, some speculation is warranted. Notably, the intensity and duration of family programming in this intervention was relatively weak. Some youth received family counseling while the parents of others participated in counseling. Youth who received family counseling demonstrated familial dysfunction sufficient to warrant increased services. Because more comprehensive services were not available in this community, traditional family counseling was employed. While family counseling has proven generally effective in other contexts (Lipsey & Wilson, 1998), more comprehensive family programming such as Functional Family Therapy (Sexton & Alexander, 2000) or Parent Management Training (Kazdin, 2005) may have been more effective than just counseling. Future research should seek to determine the effectiveness of various forms of family programming in an effort to identify which elements are successful for which groups.

Another potential explanation for the apparent lack of effectiveness of the family counseling may be related to the relatively short follow-up period associated with the current analysis. Family problems are often longstanding and difficult to ameliorate. Counseling over a longer period of time may increase the likelihood of obtaining positive results from its programming. Future analyses of these data with a longer follow-up period may shed more light on this issue.

Table 14. Bivariate Logistic Regression – Family Programming (Treatment Group; N=68)

	Official Delinquency		Self-Reported Violent		Self-Reported Nonviolent		Self-Reported Drug Use	
	Coeff.	Exp(B)	Coeff.	Exp(B)	Coeff.	Exp(B)	Coeff.	Exp(B)
Constant	-.997		.333		-.025		.201	
	(.345)		(.303)		(.298)		(.295)	
Family Programming	-.002	.998	.001	1.001	.002	1.002	-.001	.999
	(.002)		(.001)		(.001)		(.001)	
Cox & Snell R^2	.026		.022		.035		.011	
Nagelkerke R^2	.041		.030		.046		.014	

Note: standard errors in parentheses

93

Table 15. Multivariate Logistic Regression – Family Programming (Treatment Group; N=68)

	Official Delinquency		Self-Reported Violent		Self-Reported Nonviolent		Self-Reported Drug Use	
	Coeff.	Exp(B)	Coeff.	Exp(B)	Coeff.	Exp(B)	Coeff.	Exp(B)
Constant	-11.838*		-3.398		-3.382		-9.760*	
	(5.072)		(3.092)		(2.990)		(3.597)	
White	-.847	.429	-.692	.500	-.106	.900	.333	1.395
	(.682)		(.544)		(.514)		(.564)	
Male	-.465	.628	.494	.605	.690	1.993	.290	1.337
	(.755)		(.635)		(.603)		(.663)	
Age	.851*	2.341	.329	1.389	.233	1.029	.680*	1.975
	(.386)		(.242)		(.229)		(.269)	
Days in Program	.007*	1.007	-.003	.997	.000	1.000	.011*	1.011
	(.004)		(.003)		(.003)		(.004)	
Family Programming	-.001	.999	.002	1.002	.002	1.002	.000	1.000
	(.002)		(.001)		(.001)		(.001)	
Cox & Snell R^2	.167		.113		.069		.215	
Nagelkerke R^2	.257		.155		.093		.287	

Note: standard errors in parentheses; *$p < .05$ (two-tailed test)

Table 16. Self-reported Delinquency over Time by Group

	Comparison Group			Basic Treatment Group			Family Treatment Group		
	Number	*% at i1*	*% at i2*	*Number*	*% at i1*	*% at i2*	*Number*	*% at i1*	*% at i2*
Violent Offending	83	38.6	21.7***	37	86.5	62.2**	31	67.7	64.5
Nonviolent Offending	83	31.3	21.7	37	78.4	48.7***	31	58.1	64.5
Drug Use	83	10.8	8.4	37	75.7	54.1**	31	58.1	48.4

**p < .01; ***p < .001 (two-tailed test)
Values represent percent of sample reporting delinquent behaviors

HYPOTHESIS 4: CHANGE IN FAMILY BOND AND DELINQUENCY DESISTANCE

The final hypothesis tested in the current study examined the extent to which changes in strength of family bond are associated with delinquency desistance. As detailed in Chapter 3, it is hypothesized that youth who improve their relationship with their primary caretaker will be more likely to abstain from offending during the intervention. This is consistent with several theoretical perspectives that posit a negative relationship between strength of the family bond and participation in delinquent activities (see Chapter 2).

Tables 17-20 present the results of the bivariate and multivariate logistic regression models for both the treatment and comparison groups. In almost all of the models, improvement in family bond was associated with improvement in behavior. That is, youth who reported an improved relationship with their primary caretaker were less likely to self-report all forms of delinquency and drug use. The only exception to this finding emerged in the bivariate official delinquency model with the treatment group where a very small, statistically insignificant positive relationship emerged. Notably, members of the treatment group who improved their bond to their primary caretaker were significantly less likely to report involvement in nonviolent delinquency. Additional analyses (not presented) employed ordinary least squares regression using a variety measure for each of the self-reported delinquency outcomes (violent offending ranged 0-3, nonviolent offending ranged 0-8, and drug use ranged 0-4). Results were substantively similar: improvement in family bond over time translates into involvement in fewer *types* of delinquent behaviors over time.

While findings generally support Hypothesis 4, it is unclear what role the intervention played in improving relationships between child and parent among members of the treatment group. Indeed, as noted in Table 6 above, treatment and comparison youth improved at about the same rate over time.

Moreover, it is unclear whether the improvement in family bond led to improvement in behavior or whether improvement in behavior was associated with less hassles and more positive interactions with parents. It is not surprising that youth who do not report involvement in delinquency are getting along better with their parents compared to when they were involved in delinquency. Despite these potential alternative interpretations, results suggest that efforts aimed at improving family relationships may also result in the improvement of behavior over time.

ADDITIONAL ANALYSES: HIERARCHICAL LINEAR MODELING

This final stage of analysis further examines the association between family relationships and intervention success by employing Hierarchical Linear Modeling (HLM). As discussed in Chapter 3, HLM has many advantages compared to common regression approaches. In short, the method is particularly appropriate for the current study because it allows the researcher to analyze individual change over time within *and* across individuals – instead of simply changes in group means. Moreover, HLM controls for the time-dependent nature of the data. For example, time 2 delinquency is dependent on time 1 delinquency – someone who is involved in a lot of delinquent activities at time 1 is more likely to be involved in a lot of delinquent activities at time 2 than someone who has never engaged in delinquent activities. Finally, through a Bayesian estimation process, HLM can estimate difference scores for respondents who are missing time 2 data.

Table 17. Bivariate Logistic Regression – Change in Family Bond (Treatment Group; N=68)

	Official Delinquency		Self-Reported Violent		Self-Reported Nonviolent		Self-Reported Drug Use	
	Coeff.	Exp(B)	Coeff.	Exp(B)	Coeff.	Exp(B)	Coeff.	Exp(B)
Constant	-1.262		.547		.237		.058	
	(.293)		(.255)		(.258)		(.243)	
Change in Family Bond during Program	.025	1.025	-.662	.516	-1.430*	.239	-.058	.944
	(.550)		(.547)		(.576)		(.457)	
Cox & Snell R^2	.000		.027		.107		.000	
Nagelkerke R^2	.000		.037		.143		.000	

Note: standard errors in parentheses

Table 18. Multivariate Logistic Regression – Change in Family Bond (Treatment Group; N=68)

	Official Delinquency		Self-Reported Violent		Self-Reported Nonviolent		Self-Reported Drug Use	
	Coeff.	Exp(B)	Coeff.	Exp(B)	Coeff.	Exp(B)	Coeff.	Exp(B)
Constant	-12.395*		-1.729		-1.892		-9.550	
	(5.102)		(2.753)		(2.830)		(3.444)	
White	-.861	.423	-.626	.535	.013	1.013	.350	1.418
	(.679)		(.534)		(.533)		(.562)	
Male	-.382	.759	.525	1.691	.874	2.396	.337	1.400
	(.759)		(.627)		(.652)		(.673)	
Age	.876*	2.401	.213	1.237	.114	1.121	.659*	1.934
	(.387)		(.220)		(.220)		(.260)	
Days in Program	.008*	1.008	-.004	.996	.000	1.000	.011*	1.011
	(.004)		(.003)		(.003)		(.004)	
Change in Family Bond during Program	-.194	.824	-.551	.576	-1.563*	.210	-.380	.684
	(.682)		(.519)		(.620)		(.554)	
Cox & Snell R²	.165		.101		.135		.220	
Nagelkerke R²	.252		.138		.180		.293	

Note: standard errors in parentheses; *p < .05 (two-tailed test)

Table 19. Bivariate Logistic Regression – Change in Family Bond (Comparison Group; N=83)

	Self-Reported Violent		Self-Reported Nonviolent		Self-Reported Drug Use	
	Coeff.	Exp(B)	Coeff.	Exp(B)	Coeff.	Exp(B)
Constant	-1.390		-1.343		-2.677	
	(.289)		(.279)		(.495)	
Change in Family Bond Over Time	-1.633	.195	-1.150	.317	-2.426	.088
	(.874)		(.845)		(1.329)	
Cox & Snell R^2	.044		.023		.043	
Nagelkerke R^2	.068		.035		.098	

Note: standard errors in parentheses

Table 20. Multivariate Logistic Regression – Change in Family Bond (Comparison Group; N=83)

	Self-Reported Violent		Self-Reported Nonviolent		Self-Reported Drug Use	
	Coeff.	Exp(B)	Coeff.	Exp(B)	Coeff.	Exp(B)
Constant	-5.880*		-4.966		-17.051	
	(2.789)		(2.880)		(5.420)	
White	.358	1.431	.623	1.864	.535	1.707
	(.646)		(.624)		(1.044)	
Male	.832	2.298	-.308	.735	2.368	10.675
	(.615)		(.604)		(1.252)	
Age	.322	1.381	.286	1.331	.994*	2.703
	(.230)		(.240)		(.404)	
Change in Family Bond Over Time	-1.727	.178	-1.230	.292	-3.461	.031
	(.947)		(.938)		(1.851)	
Cox & Snell R^2	.094		.078		.193	
Nagelkerke R^2	.145		.120		.440	

Note: standard errors in parentheses; *p < .05 (two-tailed test)

A two-level HLM model was estimated with the first level representing two time points within individuals (initial and subsequent interviews, or pre and post; approximately 6 months between points) and the second level representing individuals (see Figure 1). Between-individual measures (level 2) in the models include: group status (delinquent or comparison), race, age, and gender. Within-individual measures (level 1) include strength of family bond and delinquency over time (measured at time 1 and time 2). As discussed at length, it is hypothesized that, as the strength of family bond increases over time, involvement in delinquent behavior will decrease. In these analyses, a variety measure of delinquency (ranging from 0 to 9) was employed representing a wide array of behaviors. Using this as the outcome variable allows for a more precise look at changes in behavior over time. Additionally, changes in strength of family bond over time will be assessed by analyzing the family bond measure as a level-one covariate. While delinquency is the outcome variable of interest throughout this study, it is also important to determine how strength of family relationships changed over time – either as a result of the intervention or not.

Difference scores were calculated for both outcome measures (delinquency and strength of family bond) by entering them as level one (within-individual) variables. In essence, this stage of the analysis estimates agreement and difference in measures at two time points (pre and post) and attempts to predict agreement and discrepancy using the salient independent variables outlined above. For example, it is hypothesized that delinquent youth will report significantly different (fewer) time 2 delinquent activities if they have a strong bond with their parents at time 1. Additionally, it is hypothesized that differences (improvement) in family bond from time 1 to time 2 are associated with differences in self-reported delinquency (improvement).

Figure 1. HLM Two-Level Model

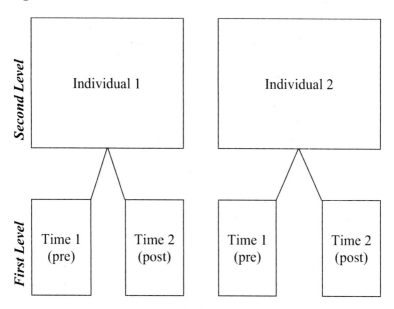

Table 21 presents the results of a basic model assessing the change in family bond over time by group status. As noted above, compared to the sample as a whole, delinquent youth start out with a significantly weaker bond to their primary caretaker (3.30 [3.53 - 0.23]). Between the first and second interview, not much changed in terms of their family bond. While statistically insignificant, and substantively small, the sample as a whole generally improved their bond with their primary caretaker (+0.01) while the bond of the delinquent youth to their primary caretakers weakened slightly (-0.02). The lack of dramatic change on measures of family bond likely relate to the relatively short period between interviews. As noted, during adolescence youth are moving away from the family and toward their peer groups as a primary source of influence. Longer time periods between interviews may be more likely to detect these changes.

Table 21. HLM: Final Estimation of Fixed Effects – Family Bond Over Time (N=217)

	Coefficient	Std. Error	t
Intercept (B0)			
Intercept (G00)	3.53	0.037	95.420***
Delinquent Group (G01)	-0.23	0.069	-3.296***
Slope (time – B1)			
Intercept (G10)	0.01	0.037	0.36
Delinquent Group (G11)	-0.02	0.072	-0.26

*p < .05; **p < .01; ***p < .001 (two-tailed test)

Table 22. HLM: Final Estimation of Fixed Effects – Family Bond Over Time (N=217)

	Coefficient	Std. Error	t
Intercept (B0)			
Intercept (G00)	1.11	0.110	10.08***
Delinquent Group (G01)	2.41	0.260	9.26***
Slope (time – B1)			
Intercept (G10)	-0.40	0.101	-3.95***
Delinquent Group (G11)	-0.52	0.270	-1.92

*p < .05; **p < .01; ***p < .001 (two-tailed test)

Table 22 presents the results of the basic model assessing change in self-reported delinquent behavior over time by group status. At the first interview, the combined sample reported participating in an average of about one delinquent activity (1.11), however, members of the delinquent group reported significantly more participation (about 3.52 behaviors [1.11 = 2.41]). Between interview 1 and interview 2, on average the whole sample decreased the number of delinquent activities in which they were involved. In addition, delinquent youth reported a more dramatic decrease. Specifically, at time 2 the sample as a whole reported engaging in about 0.71 types of offenses (1.11 – 0.40). Delinquent youth reported participating in about 3.00 (3.52 - .52) offenses at time 2.

Table 23. HLM: Final Estimation of Fixed Effects – Demographic Controls and Variety of Delinquent Activities (N=217)

	Coefficient	Std. Error	t
Intercept (B0)			
Intercept (G00)	-2.96	1.217	-2.43*
Delinquent Group (G01)	2.22	0.263	8.45***
White (G02)	-0.62	0.230	-2.68**
Male (G03)	0.49	0.224	2.17*
Age (G04)	0.34	0.010	3.39***
Slope (time – B1)			
Intercept (G10)	-0.59	1.115	-0.53
Delinquent Group (G11)	-0.58	0.260	-2.23*
White (G12)	0.87	0.270	3.01**
Male (G13)	0.09	0.268	0.33
Age (G14)	-0.02	0.090	-0.18

*p < .05; **p < .01; ***p < .001 (two-tailed test)

Table 23 presents the results of a basic HLM model testing the influence of demographic variables in predicting delinquent behaviors (a variety score) over time. Specifically, time and delinquency were entered at level 1 (within individual) and group status (treatment or comparison), race (white), gender (male), and age were entered at level 2 (between individual). At the first interview, delinquent youth reported more delinquency than comparison youth, white youth reported more delinquency than nonwhite youth, males reported more delinquency than females, and older youth reported participation in more delinquent behaviors than younger respondents. Between the first and second interview, the group as a whole decreased offending, while delinquent youth reported an even more significant decrease (-0.58). White youth increased offending over time (0.87 increase in the number of offenses compared to -

0.59 for the group as a whole). While statistically insignificant, males did not decrease offending as much as females and older youth reported fewer delinquent activities than younger youth.

Table 24 presents the results of the Hierarchical Linear Modeling analysis predicting change in delinquency by group status (treatment or comparison) and with strength of family bond at interview 1 entered at level 2. As a whole, the sample engaged in an average of 3.81 different delinquent acts. The delinquent youth engaged in an average of 2.23 additional types of offenses than the group as a whole. Additionally, for every unit increase in strength of family bond at interview 1, youth engaged in 0.76 *fewer* types of offenses. Over time, youth engaged in 1.36 fewer types of offenses. Delinquent youth engaged in *even fewer* types of offenses (-0.46). Finally, for each unit increase in family bond at interview 1, youth engaged in fewer types of offenses, but this decrease was not as dramatic as the sample as a whole (1.09 decrease over time [-1.36-.27]). Because respondents who have a strong family bond start out committing fewer types of offenses, it appears that they do not decrease as much as the others.

Table 24. HLM: Final Estimation of Fixed Effects – Family Bond at Time 1 and Variety of Delinquent Activities (N=217)

	Coefficient	Std. Error	t
Intercept (B0)			
Intercept (G00)	3.81	0.852	4.46***
Delinquent Group (G01)	2.23	0.236	9.45***
Mean Family Bond at i1 (G02)	-0.76	0.238	-3.21**
Slope (time – B1)			
Intercept (G10)	-1.36	0.958	-1.42
Delinquent Group (G11)	-0.46	0.262	-1.76
Mean Family Bond at i1 (G12)	0.27	0.264	1.04

**p < .01; ***p < .001 (two-tailed test)

Figure 2 graphically depicts the findings from Table 24. Notably, delinquent youth start out participating in a wider variety of offenses than the group as a whole, and decrease more dramatically over time. Because they start out committing significantly more types of delinquent activities, they still reported more types of offending at time 2 than the group as a whole. Youth who report a strong bond to their parent at time 1 (graphically presented as a one unit increase) start out committing fewer types of offenses, and decrease in variety over time, but not as considerably as the sample as a whole.

Figure 2. HLM: Discrepancy within Individuals over Time (Family Bond at Time 1)

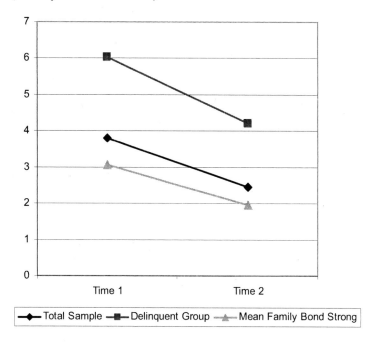

Table 25 presents the results of an HLM model estimating the within-individual relationship between change in family bond and delinquency over time by group status. Specifically, time and mean family bond were entered as level-one predictors and group status (delinquent or comparison) was entered as a level-two predictor of self-reported delinquency (a level-one outcome variable). As expected, delinquent youth reported participation in a greater variety of delinquent offenses at time 1 (2.88 more than the group as a whole). In addition, over time delinquent youth reported a more dramatic decrease in the number of delinquent activities participated in during the follow-up period, however they still reported a wider variety of offenses than youth in the comparison group. Finally, youth who reported increases in the strength of the family bond over time were more likely to report fewer types of delinquent offenses over time. Again, decreases were more dramatic (though not significantly different) for delinquent youth. While these results are similar to what was found using logistic regression models, the HLM more clearly demonstrates the differences between the delinquent and comparison groups.

Table 25. HLM: Final Estimation of Fixed Effects – Family Bond Change over Time and Variety of Delinquent Activities (N=217)

	Coefficient	Std. Error	t
Intercept (B0)			
Intercept (G00)	2.54	0.610	4.167***
Delinquent Group (G01)	2.88	0.993	2.897**
Slope (time – B2)			
Intercept (G20)	-0.39	0.096	-4.11***
Delinquent Group (G21)	-0.56	0.264	-2.14*
Slope (mean family bond – B1)			
Intercept (G10)	-0.41	0.160	-2.57*
Delinquent Group (G11)	-0.17	0.271	-0.62

**p < .01; ***p < .001 (two-tailed test)

Results from the HLM analysis largely replicate earlier findings but also suggest that delinquent youth improved their behavior more dramatically than comparison youth. While this may simply be a function of regression to the mean, it also may be indicative of some success on the part of the intervention. That is, over time a greater proportion of youth who were involved in the intervention desisted offending. Moreover, strength of family bond was important in determining delinquent involvement at time 1 and time 2. Specifically, youth who reported a stronger bond to their parent at time 1 reported participation in fewer types of delinquent behavior at that time than youth who were not strongly bonded to their parent. Also, improvement in family bond over time was associated with improvement in behavior; that is, youth who improved their relationship over time reported participation in fewer types of delinquent behaviors.

CHAPTER 5
Discussion and Conclusion

While findings from the current study are equivocal, they do provide some insight into the effect of a strong family bond on successful delinquency desistance in a specific intervention setting. First, a general inverse relationship emerged between strength of family bond upon beginning the intervention and subsequent delinquency. That is, while largely statistically insignificant, youth who began the intervention with a strong bond to their primary caretaker were less likely to offend during and immediately following the intervention. This relationship also emerged, however, for the comparison group of youth who were not involved in the intervention, suggesting the program may have added little to the dynamic between family bond and delinquency.

Additionally, youth who reported improvement in their family bond over time were also less likely to report involvement in delinquent behavior over time. Because improvement in family relationships occurred concomitantly with improvement in behavior, targeting family dynamics appears to be an effective strategy to reduce involvement in delinquent behavior. Whether this relationship is direct or indirect, findings from the current study indicate that focusing on strengthening family relationships may result in decreased involvement in delinquency. In the current study, however, the effect appeared

111

to be more indirect; that is, the family programming component did not appear to directly impact involvement in delinquency.

Results from the current study also add to the sizeable literature that explores the relationship between family structure and delinquency. Taken together, results again are largely unclear. There were no statistically significant results indicating two parents were better than one; indeed, a higher proportion of treatment youth who lived in a two-parent household were arrested within 6 months and reported involvement in violent and nonviolent delinquency. Among the comparison group, results were mixed and also statistically insignificant. Recent research has suggested that measuring family structure as simply a one- or two-parent household may mask important differences that may exist within different households (Demuth & Brown, 2004; Kierkus & Baer, 2003). For example, a male guardian may be different than a female guardian depending on the gender of the child. Moreover, households with a nonbiological second parent may not necessarily be better than single-parent households. Again, the quality of the parent-child relationship appeared to be more salient (Sokol-Katz et al., 1997; Van Voorhis et al., 1988).

The current study also failed to uncover promising results for youth who received family counseling. As discussed above, the ineffectiveness of the family counseling may be attributed to several processes. First, the family counseling may not have been comprehensive enough to improve family relationships among youth in the sample. Lipsey and Wilson's (1998) meta-analysis of effective interventions for serious offenders revealed that family counseling was among the programs that were moderately effective. While we know that youth and/or parents were counseled by trained facilitators with MSW degrees, it is unclear the specific nature of the family counseling employed in the current intervention. Future research evaluating the effectiveness of family programs ought to determine exactly what methods are being used by counselors to better identify the type of family counseling that is most effective.

Second, the counseling may take a long period of time to produce the desired effects. Family problems are often long-standing and difficult to fix quickly. Since the current study employed a relatively short follow-up period (approximately 6 months), changes may not yet be measurable. Additional follow-ups with this sample may better assess the long-term effect of the family counseling, and future studies should employ multiple follow-up periods (both short- and long-term if possible). There are several theoretical and policy implications stemming from this study that will be highlighted next.

THEORETICAL IMPLICATIONS

In general, results of the current study are supportive of theoretical perspectives that place importance on the quality of the relationship between parent and child. As reviewed in Chapter 2, several theoretical formulations argue for the delinquency-inhibiting properties of the parent-child bond. Youth in both the comparison and treatment groups who reported stronger bonds to their parent were less likely to report involvement in delinquent behaviors. This finding remained consistent both contemporaneously and longitudinally. That is, the stronger the strength of family bond at interview 1, the less likely the youth reported involvement in delinquent behavior at interview 1 and interview 2.

Results from the current study also provide evidence that emotional attachment may be more salient than family structure. While the emotional bond measures were related to delinquency in the theoretically expected direction in all of the models, family structure was inconsistently and in some cases opposite of what was expected. Previous research has suggested, however, that attachment and structure may be related. Sokol-Katz and associates (1997) found that family structure was significantly related to family attachment which had a significant and direct effect on minor and serious delinquency and drug, alcohol, and tobacco use (Sokol-Katz et al., 1997). These researchers, therefore, concluded that individuals who are firmly tied to a "broken" or reconstituted (remarried) family are less likely to engage in deviant activities than individuals unattached to intact families; level of attachment proved more salient than structure of family (Sokol-Katz et al., 1997). On the other hand, Thornberry and colleagues (1999) argue that transitions that occur as a result of changes in family structure are associated with a variety of negative outcomes.

These findings are especially important because little empirical attention has been devoted to testing theoretical tenets among samples of children in general and serious young offenders in particular. As expected, the family appears especially important among this specialized population. Thornberry (1987:873) stresses the importance of family during the preadolescent years: "During the early adolescent years, the family is the most salient arena for social interaction and involvement and, because of this, attachment to parents has a stronger influence on other aspects of the youth's life at this stage than it does at later stages of development." Future research ought to continue this trend by testing other criminological perspectives using samples of offenders at various developmental stages.

POLICY IMPLICATIONS

In the early 1970's, many researchers concluded that "nothing works" to rehabilitate offenders, particularly serious, violent, and/or chronic offenders (Martinson, 1974). Gottfredson and Hirschi (1990:268) summarize this position aptly: "Among academicians, the conclusion that rehabilitation programs have been extensively tried and have been found wanting is generally accepted." As a result, many advocated for a more deterrence-based approach focusing on incarceration programs to keep communities safe (Martinson, 1974; Whitehead & Lab, 1989; see also Gibbons, 1999 or Palmer, 1991 for a historical review). Since then, however, a wealth of knowledge has been accumulated that suggests many programs do work for certain offenders under certain circumstances and in certain situations (Andrews et al., 1990; Cullen, 2005; Palmer, 1991, 1995; Sherman et al., 1997; Wasserman, Miller, & Cothern, 2000). Howell (1995:158) summarizes this sentiment: "It can be said with confidence that some programs do work when they are carefully conceived, properly implemented, and provided with enough resources to do the job they set out to do."

The current study revealed that interventions that simply add-on family counseling may not be as effective as more comprehensive family-based programming that is central to the intervention. At least in the short-term, youth who received family counseling were no less likely to report involvement in delinquency than youth who did not participate in family counseling. Program administrators acknowledged that rehabilitating family relationships was not the primary focus of this particular intervention, although they recognized the importance of such programming. As a result, findings presented here should not be misinterpreted as evidence against the use of family-focused programming. Indeed, they may be interpreted as a call for more comprehensive family-oriented approaches.

A highlight of the current intervention was the commitment to keep youth in their familial environments as much as possible. This was more easily facilitated by employing a unique intensive supervision program that organized probation officers around specific neighborhoods. This approach allowed probation officers to coordinate supervision activities with community police officers and other neighborhood institutions (e.g., school officials, neighborhood groups, churches). In the current program, community police officers often joined probation officers on their rounds and pointed out characteristics of the environment (such as potential resources) or of the particular family (such as relatives known to police) that the probation officer may not have known. Other jurisdictions ought to consider this approach as it appeared to aid in the overall continuum of care offered to participants.

There are also several recommendations for future research stemming from lessons learned during this project. First, it would be interesting to collect data from caretakers regarding their perceptions of the relationship they have with their child. Is there agreement among parents and children regarding the quality of the relationship? Perhaps parents feel that they have a good relationship with their child, but children do not share this perception. Furthermore, future studies ought to consider questioning youth about any other potential influences in their lives (secondary caretakers). A strong bond to a teacher or mentor may have the same power as that with a parent.

Second, it is important that program evaluators collect specific data regarding programming. While this study was able to analyze the number of minutes of family programming received, it was unable to clearly discern differences that may have existed in terms of the quality of the family counseling in the current program compared to others. Finally, it is imperative that future studies randomly assign participants to a treatment or control condition such that any differences between the two groups can be more clearly attributed to the treatment program.

CHARACTERISTICS OF SUCCESSFUL INTERVENTIONS

After reviewing over 500 intervention evaluations, Lipsey (1999:564) concluded that "...well designed rehabilitative strategies do reduce recidivism for [the most serious offenders] and cannot be dismissed on the grounds that they are ineffective." Indeed, Martinson has even tempered his earlier argument that 'nothing works', suggesting that some programs have demonstrated desired results (Martinson, 1979). Despite the mounting body of supportive research and overwhelming public support for early intervention (Cullen et al., 1998; Moon, Sundt, Cullen, & Wright, 2000), it has only been relatively recently that interventions have been developed, implemented, and evaluated which target early offenders.

As noted above, family-based or family-focused interventions have routinely demonstrated more effectiveness than non-family interventions (Dowden & Andrews, 2003; Latimer, 2001; Perkins-Dock, 2001). For example, Kazdin (1987) argued that family interventions hold the most promise for the treatment of Conduct Disorder in children and adolescents. Moreover, parent-focused interventions implemented at home or in other community locations tend to be very successful (Burns et al., 2003). Finally, Gavazzi, Yarcheck, Rhine, and Partridge (2003) advocate a family-based parole program guided by lessons learned from restorative justice practices. In short, there are several specific family oriented interventions that have proven effective in a range of situations with a variety of juvenile offenders. Functional family therapy, parent management training, and multisystemic therapy are examples of comprehensive interventions that incorporate parental components and have proven effective at reducing delinquent behavior among serious juvenile offenders.

Functional Family Therapy

Functional Family Therapy (FFT) focuses on parent-child communication and employs behavioral contracting, clear specification of rules, and a token economy (Tarolla et al., 2002). In behavioral contracting, the child signs a contract in which prosocial behaviors are linked with rewards while specific punishments are prescribed for the violation of rules such as loss of allowance for theft (Pearson, Lipton, Cleland, & Yee, 2002). A token reinforcement system involves providing rewards to children or families for displaying desirable behaviors (Pearson et al., 2002).

Typically, Functional Family Therapy consists of 12 1-hour sessions over the course of 3 months; difficult cases may require more dosage or duration. In the first phase of FFT (induction-motivation or engagement), therapists attempt to reframe conflicted family interactions to foster a less threatening environment in which to begin treatment (Robbins, Alexander, & Turner, 2000). Specifically, therapists use reframing to "...immediately disrupt or alter negative family interactions to prevent the family from dropping out of treatment" (Robbins et al., 2000:689). Robbins and colleagues (2000) found that therapists who employed reframing in the initial session saw significantly decreased defensive behaviors by families than therapists who used other approaches (e.g., reflection, elicit-structure).

In the second phase of FFT (behavioral change), therapists develop and implement developmentally appropriate short, intermediate, and long-term treatment plans for each member of the family (Sexton & Alexander, 2000). Finally, in phase three (generalization), clinicians apply lessons learned to other areas of family functioning. Sexton and Alexander (2000:4) point out that the goal of this final stage is "to improve a family's ability to affect the multiple systems in which it is embedded (e.g., school, juvenile justice system, community), thereby allowing the family to mobilize community support systems and modify deteriorating family-system relationships." As such, families are referred to appropriate community resources to ensure that progress made in FFT sessions continues when the therapist discontinues regular meetings.

Several evaluations have demonstrated that Functional Family Therapy can be effective in treating antisocial youth in dysfunctional family settings (Gordon, Graves, & Arbuthnot, 1995; Klein, Alexander, & Parsons, 1977; Perkins-Dock, 2001; Sexton & Alexander, 2000). For example, Gordon, Arbuthnot, Gustafson, and McGreen (1988) evaluated a Functional Family Therapy program with strong behavioral and social learning components. They found that, compared to traditional probation, the family therapy group recidivated much less after 30 months (11% compared to 67%; Gordon et al., 1988). Of the 80% of participants who completed the full course of treatment in a large

FFT program (a very impressive completion rate), less than 20% committed an offense within one year, compared to almost twice that rate for a control group (Mihalic, Irwin, Elliott, Fagan, & Hansen, 2001). Functional Family Therapy is also cost-effective: treatment cost is usually between $1,000-3,000 per family, compared to $6,000 for detention and $13,500 for residential treatment for the same period (Alexander et al., 1998; Mihalic et al., 2001).

Parent Management Training

Parent Management Training (PMT) is informed by social learning and coercion theory and teaches parents effective communication techniques, nonviolent disciplinary tactics (such as time out or loss of privileges), and other problem solving skills so that they are enabled to effectively modify their child's negative behavior (Perkins-Dock, 2001). Treatment is usually administered individually or among a group of parents in a school or clinical setting. Parents are taught to resist physical punishment and encourage prosocial behavior using rewards or other privileges (Wasserman & Seracini, 2001).

Evaluation of PMT appears promising: most program families demonstrate significant improvements in parent-child relations and decreased out-of-home placements while youth exhibit reductions in delinquent behaviors, substance use, and associations with deviant peers (Kazdin, 1997; Kazdin, 2005; Kazdin, Siegel, & Bass, 1992; Serketich & Dumas, 1996). Moreover, combined with general problem-solving skills training, PMT has proven effective among severely antisocial youths (Kazdin et al., 1992). Long-term effect on delinquency prevention, however, is still largely unclear (Wasserman & Miller, 1998) and some questions have been raised about its effectiveness among families living in poverty (Eamon & Venkataraman, 2003) and families with foreign-born parents (Martinez and Eddy, 2005; but see also Ho, Chow, & Fung, 1999).

Multisystemic Therapy

Multisystemic Therapy (MST) moves beyond traditional family therapy in that it considers the ecological nature of adolescent development (Bronfrenbrenner, 1979; see also Tolan, Guerra, & Kendall, 1995). Specifically, it is argued that dysfunctions in any system, family, peer group, community, or school, can result in antisocial behavior by the individual. Tate and colleagues note that "MST interventions are child-focused, family-centered, and directed toward solving multiple problems across the numerous contexts in which the youth is embedded: family, peers, school, and neighborhood" (Tate, Reppucci, & Mulvey, 1995:779). Similarly, changes in one domain may or may not result in system-wide changes. Mihalic and associates (2001) also observe that the primary aim of MST is to give parents tools to help their children deal with problems that arise in other social domains such that out-of-home placements become unnecessary. MST identifies and attempts to break down potential barriers to functional family relationships, such as parental drug abuse and physical abuse or neglect. By working from within the family, MST seeks to provide a supportive environment to address other problems at school, with peers, or in other areas of the adolescent's life. Working with the family, a therapist develops a comprehensive treatment plan that includes family therapy, cognitive-behavioral treatment, parent training, or a host of other developmentally appropriate interventions. MST typically continues for 4 months with an average of 60 hours of therapist contact over the course of that time period. Treatment is usually delivered in a community location (typically the family's home) to reduce resistance to participation. Sessions are conducted as often as daily and as infrequently as once a week, depending on the current stage of treatment.

MST has proven successful with a variety of antisocial offenders, including substance abusers, sex offenders, suicidal adolescents, inner-city youth, and serious juvenile offenders (Borduin, 1994; Borduin et al., 1995; Henggeler, 1996, 1997;

Henggeler, Melton, & Smith, 1992). Moreover, evaluations have revealed reductions in short and long-term arrests (up to 4 years following treatment) and out-of-home placements for adolescents (Mihalic et al., 2001). Henggeler and colleagues (1992) examined the efficacy of family preservation-based MST for serious juvenile offenders in South Carolina. Using a rigorous methodology (pretest-posttest control groups with random assignment), these researchers found that compared to a control group sentenced to traditional probation, MST participants self-reported significantly fewer delinquent behaviors, fewer arrests, and fewer weeks of incarceration following the intervention (Henggeler et al., 1992). Henggeler and associates (1992:958) concluded that "...findings support the effectiveness of family preservation using MST, relative to usual services, in reducing the institutionalization of serious juvenile offenders and in attenuating their criminal activity." Additionally, their results suggest that MST can be equally as effective for a wide variety of individual and family characteristics (they controlled for race, age, social class, gender, criminal history, family and peer relations, social competence, behavioral problems, and parent symptomatology).

Henggeler and colleagues (1992) also demonstrated that MST can be effectively implemented in a community setting. The researchers provided only modest training to therapists prior to beginning the project, supplemented with weekly phone communications and booster training sessions every two months. This relatively little involvement appeared to maintain treatment fidelity such that promising findings emerged. Finally, MST is relatively cost effective. The average cost per client for the course of the MST intervention (about 3 months) was approximately $2,800—significantly less than the average institutional placement ($16,300). Henggeler et al. (1992) maintain: "...it is clear that MST, while substantially more effective, is much less expensive than usual services" (see also Tate et al., 1995; Mihalic et al., 2001:10).

The above-referenced programs have proven effective in intervening with serious juvenile delinquents in a variety of contexts. The specific program employed, however, will vary depending on the problems exhibited by the youth (as evidenced in a comprehensive risk and needs assessment). For instance, a youth with few family problems will require fewer resources devoted to the family (e.g., occasional family counseling) whereas youth experiencing family-centered crises require more intensive family programming such as family preservation or even temporary out-of-home placement (such as therapeutic foster care). In general, however, most youth and their families will benefit from the basic services provided through Functional Family Therapy or multisystemic therapy (Mihalic et al., 2001). As noted by Smith and Stern (1997:406), "*early* intervention is the key, given the relative stability of early aggressive behavior and its relationship to delinquency, and a social learning approach incorporating parent training in family management strategies has demonstrated efficacy" (emphasis in original).

LIMITATIONS OF THE CURRENT STUDY

While this analysis has contributed to the overall body of evidence concerning interventions that target serious childhood delinquents, it is not without limitations. A primary concern with the current analyses is the size of the sample. While a small number of serious juvenile offenders is good for society, it is problematic for statistical analyses. Even though some statistically significant findings emerged, the results must be interpreted with caution and, overall, generalizability is questioned due to the small number of individuals in the study.

Another notable limitation of the current study is the lack of a control group of offenders who did not participate in the intervention. Indeed, the ideal method would have involved the random assignment of delinquent youth to either the program or a control condition. Due to the relative scarcity of youth under the age of 14 who participate in serious delinquency, there were not enough youth to assign to different conditions. As a result, it is difficult to accurately ascertain the influence of the intervention on the treatment youth with regard to the strength of their family bond.

Moreover, the comparison group employed was one of convenience, and may not represent the attitudes, beliefs, and behaviors of "normally" developing preadolescents. While efforts were made to recruit a representative sample of youth (by supplementing youth from a middle school with youth from two recreation centers in the target area), sample selection bias is a potential problem. Because active consent was required for participation in the study, youth interested in participating were required to obtain permission via a signed form from a parent. Biases may have been introduced as a function of those parents willing to consent and return the signed form to researchers on time.

As noted, there are substantial differences between the comparison and treatment groups that limit the ability of the findings to definitively answer the research question posed. Specifically, the two groups were not equal in terms of their family relationships at the first interview. It is interesting to note, however, that even though the comparison youth started out with significantly stronger bonds to their primary caretaker, they changed at about the same rate as the delinquent youth.

Sample attrition is another limitation of the current study. As presented in Chapter 3, there were significant differences between youth who were successfully re-interviewed and those who were not. This was especially striking for the comparison group. While every effort was made to interview all treatment and comparison youth at two time periods, many families moved out of the area or were otherwise unreachable. As a result, selection-mortality may threaten internal validity of the data analyzed in the current study.

Another potential limitation of the study is the reliance on self-reported data. While official delinquency was used as an outcome measure for the treatment youth, self-reported measures of family bond and delinquency were the primary variables employed in the study. With regard to strength of the family bond, youth may have different perceptions about this relationship than parents. It would be interesting and important to ask parents the same questions about their children to determine the extent of agreement.

Social scientists recognize that self-report measures of delinquency have notable sources of error (Maxfield et al., 2000). For example, some respondents may be more or less likely to report offending to researchers in certain circumstances (experimenter effect). In addition, respondents who are surveyed multiple times may be influenced by previous interviews (panel effect). It has also been argued that self-reports do not measure serious delinquency, are not standardized, and are invalid (Hindelang, Hirschi, & Weis, 1981). While these latter concerns are arguably less applicable to recent survey designs, questions still exist as to the extent to which youth will honestly report deviant (especially serious) offenses.

Self-report data seem to better measure minor deviances such as smoking, truancy, and marijuana use because these offenses are often not captured in official records (Elliott & Ageton, 1980). Similarly, a respondent may be less likely to report a very serious offense (sexual assault, robbery) to a survey researcher but there is more likelihood these offenses will emerge in official data – especially if the youth is a repeat or chronic offender (Elliott & Ageton, 1980). Because of the strengths and limitations associated with self-report and official sources of data, both were used independently as outcome measures in an effort to broaden generalizability.

The face-to-face interviewing approach employed in the current study has several strengths. Indeed, this approach is among the most highly regarded in social science research (Singleton & Straits, 1999). First, interviewers were able to clarify questions that respondents were unclear about. This proved especially important considering the target population – youth between the ages of 10 and 13. Even though the research staff attempted to develop an interview instrument that was easily understandable and based on previously used questions, some of the younger respondents had difficulty understanding concepts such as "criticize" or even "unlikely" and still others did not know what "ecstasy" or "a rave" was. Trained interviewers were able to explain these concepts to youth in an effort to elicit the most accurate response to any given question.

Second, sensitive or uncomfortable questions cannot be overlooked by respondents as easily when interviewed in person as compared to self-administered questionnaires. Even though respondents were not pressured into answering questions they were uncomfortable about, very few missing values were present in these data.

One problem associated with face-to-face interviews, however, is the potential for bias to be introduced (either explicitly or implicitly) by the individual interviewer. For example, female youth may respond differently to male interviewers than female interviewers. Respondents may answer questions differently depending on the race of the interviewer compared to that of their own. Finally, different interviewers may phrase questions a bit differently or inadvertently look intently at respondents when asking them about delinquent activities. All of these issues are potentially damaging to any social scientific effort using face-to-face interviews, however, good training of interviewers can limit their negative effect. The current study attempted to limit interviewer bias by training each interviewer, systematizing instructions to by read by interviewers to respondents, and, when possible, having female researchers interview female youth and male researchers interview male youth.

Another concern that has been leveled by researchers regarding self-report studies is the extent to which youth may exaggerate, forget, or lie about their activities. Of particular concern with face-to-face interviews is the extent to which respondents will be completely honest with their responses. This concern is especially appropriate given the types of questions asked in surveys of delinquent behavior. As with all research using this methodology, respondents were reassured several times throughout the interview session that their individual responses would be protected to the maximum extent allowable by law.

As a final measure to assess the truthfulness of respondents, at the end of the study they were asked "While you were answering the interviewer's questions, how truthful were your responses?" After the first interview, 81% of youth answered "very truthful" and an additional 18% responded "somewhat truthful." Concluding the second interview, 85% of youth responded "very truthful" while an additional 14% responded "somewhat truthful." While this is a rudimentary assessment of the truthfulness of respondents, it does provide an additional level of confidence in the answers obtained.

CONCLUSION

Early offending is a paradox for justice professionals. Police officers do not know how do handle young delinquents, resulting in many needy youth slipping through the proverbial cracks. Minor deviance such as truancy, substance use, and fighting is ubiquitous during adolescence; however, these same behaviors exhibited earlier (at 6-11 years of age) are potent risk factors for continued involvement in delinquency. Police officers and juvenile justice professionals must be prepared to address the causes of early offending. In its current state, the juvenile justice system can offer little in the way of services to this small but difficult population. Mental health officials are in a better position to provide for these families, yet are often kept "out of the loop." A partnership must be forged between state and local mental health and juvenile justice officials in a cooperative attack on child delinquency. Approaches that avoid the formal stigma of the juvenile court are preferred, yet officials must ensure treatment plans are followed. The evidence is convincing that failure to intervene with children who initiate offending at an early age may result in a population of serious, violent, and chronic juvenile and adult offenders.

Results of this study are important for a number of reasons. First, findings presented support theoretical perspectives that argue for the delinquency inhibiting properties of a strong bond to parents. In almost all models for both the delinquent and comparison youth, respondents who reported a stronger relationship with their parent were less likely to report involvement in delinquency. Second, family structure does not appear to be an important predictor of delinquency desistance for most youth. Program administrators cannot simply assume that youth who reside with two parents are going to demand fewer familial services than youth residing with only one parent. Third, the family programming employed in the current intervention appeared, at least in the immediate short-term, ineffective at reducing involvement in delinquent behaviors. Future interventions must incorporate more rigorous forms of family-based programming such as functional family therapy or parent management training and employ a longer follow-up period to determine long-term outcomes of the treatment.

Program administrators must continue to employ innovative treatment approaches that are theoretically grounded and empirically supported. Moreover, comprehensive process and outcome evaluations must be associated with these efforts so that results of promising and proven programs can be propagated and programs replicated in various settings with diverse populations of offenders. While results from the current study were mixed, they help to advance the field incrementally by identifying what aspects of programming are effective (and ineffective) at improving the behavior of serious, violent, juvenile offenders.

Despite the wealth of promising evidence in favor of community-based programs, little has changed in the juvenile justice system. Most jurisdictions still largely rely on incapacitation and surveillance approaches to manage serious, violent, and chronic offenders. In many cases, the problem is not that multisystemic therapy or similar strategies are too costly.

Indeed, most community-based interventions are much less expensive than detention or other out-of-home placement options. What is needed, in short, is a paradigm shift. Legislatures must fund treatment-based alternatives to incarceration; practitioners must implement empirically-supported and theoretically meaningful programs; and researchers must rigorously evaluate existing and innovative interventions. The current study represents a small step in this direction.

Survey Instrument

Michigan Juvenile Intervention Initiative

Michigan State University is conducting a research project designed to determine the extent of needs among arrested juveniles in Michigan. The project is intended to learn more about the individuals who are arrested in order to design more effective delinquency intervention programs.

You need to know that your participation in this project is entirely voluntary. The project includes two interviews and collection of official data including: your school records; official police records; Social Services files; and court records. You do not have to participate in any facet of the project. Your signed consent form will permit project staff to have access to these records for the duration of your participation in the project.

We anticipate that this interview will take 20 minutes. You do not have to participate. If you choose to participate, you can refuse to answer any of the questions and you can stop the interview at any time. If you refuse to participate in the interview, or to answer specific questions, no one will know of your refusal. The interview process consists of two sessions, with a second interview in six to twelve months. Participation in the second interview is entirely voluntary and you may discontinue involvement in the project at any time.

All information received is considered confidential. The data we collect will not include your name or any information that could identify you. Your privacy will be protected to the maximum extent allowable by law. If you would like more information, we will provide a document regarding the Confidentiality of Information.

   This interview is not at all related to your arrest. Your willingness, or refusal, to participate will in no way effect your case in any court, nor will anyone in the legal system know of your participation or refusal to participate. By proceeding with this interview you are indicating your voluntary participation with this project.

If you have any further questions about this project, please contact either:

Michigan State University
School of Criminal Justice
560 Baker Hall
East Lansing, MI 48824
517-355-2197

or

University Committee on Research Involving Human Subjects
Michigan State University
246 Administrative Building
East Lansing, MI 48824-1046
517-355-2180

Youth Participant Printed Name_____

Youth Participant Signature _____

Parent/Guardian Printed Name_____

Parent/Guardian Signature_____

MICHIGAN JUVENILE INTERVENTION INITIATIVE
ASSESSMENT
REVISED VERSION (06-06-02)

FIRST INTERVIEW

Youth Last Name _____ **MSU ID#** _____

Youth First Name _____

Interview Date _____

Interview Number   1   2   3

Site: FL   GR   LAN   SAG

Interviewer _____

Sample Youth   ☐
Control Youth   ☐

ENTRY_____
DATE_____

Directions to be read to juvenile.
I am from Michigan State University, and am not in any way working for the police, the schools, or any other agency in the city. We are looking to gather information about youth to better understand why they sometimes get into trouble. Your individual responses will be protected to the maximum extent allowable by law.

I am going to read you some statements about your attitudes towards certain behaviors, school, and your beliefs about events in your life. Think about each statement I make and then tell me if you Strongly Agree with the statement, Agree with the statement, Disagree with the statement, or Strongly Disagree with the statement. If you are not sure, give the response that is closest to how you feel about the statement I make.

(Provide response card # 1 to the juvenile).
☐ Strongly Agree ☐ Agree ☐ Disagree ☐ Strongly Disagree

(i1wai)
1. I'm not very sure of myself.
2. I really don't like myself very much.
3. I sometimes feel so bad about myself that I wish I were somebody else.
4. I usually feel I'm the kind of person I want to be.
5. I feel I can do things as well as other people can.
6. I feel that I am a special or important person.
7. I feel that I am really good at things I try to do.

(i1ipfi)
1. Other people decide what happens to me.
2. It is important to think before you act.
3. If I study, I will get better grades.
4. When I try to be nice, people notice.
5. If you work hard, you will get what you want.
6. To make a good decision, it is important to think.
7. I am responsible for what happens to me.
8. Sometimes you have to physically fight to get what you want.
9. I get mad easy.
10. I do whatever I feel like doing.
11. When I get mad, I yell at people.
12. Sometimes I break things on purpose.

13. If I feel like it, I hit people.

(i1bsa)

1. It makes you feel big and tough when you push someone around.
2. If you back down from a fight, everyone will think you are a coward.
3. Sometimes you have only two choices – get punched or punch the other kid first.
4. It's OK to hit someone if you just go crazy with anger.
5. A guy who doesn't fight back when other kids push him around will lose respect.
6. A guy shows he really loves his girlfriend if he gets in fights with other guys about her.

(i1atv)

1. If I walk away from a fight, I'd be a coward ("chicken").
2. I don't need to fight because there are other ways to deal with being mad.
3. It's ok to hit someone who hits you first.
4. If a kid teases me, I usually cannot get him/her to stop unless I hit him/her.
5. If I refuse to fight, my friends will think I'm afraid.

(i1atg)

1. I think you are safer, and have protection, if you join a gang.
2. I will probably join a gang.
3. Some of my friends at school belong to gangs.
4. My friends would think less of me if I joined a gang.
5. I believe it is dangerous to join a gang; you will probably end up getting hurt or killed if you belong to a gang.
6. I think being in a gang makes it more likely that you will get into trouble.
7. Some people in my family belong to a gang, or used to belong to a gang.
8. I belong to a gang.

(i1ats)

1. Homework is a waste of time.
2. I try hard in school.

3. Education is so important that it's worth it to put up with things about school that I don't like.
4. In general, I like school.
5. I don't care what teachers think of me.
6. I expect to graduate from High School.
7. I expect to go to college.
8. I expect that my education will influence my future success.

Directions to be read to juvenile. I have a few more questions about school. I am going to ask you about your involvement in activities that take place in school. Think about this year and tell me if you Always, Sometimes, Once in a While, or Never are involved in these school activities.

(Provide response card # 2 to the juvenile).
□ Never □ Once in a While □ Sometimes □ Always

9. During the school year I do my homework.
10. During the school year I participate in school sports besides gym.
11. During the school year I belong to clubs or organizations in the school.
12. During the school year I skip classes
13. During the school year I get help with my homework from a teacher or tutor

(il paid)
Directions to be read to juvenile. I am going to read you some statements about what your closest friends think about some behaviors. Think about all the people you hung around with in the past year, including your two or three closest friends. Tell me how your friends would respond to some situations in terms of Strongly Approving, Approving, Disapproving, or Strongly Disapproving of the behavior.

(Provide response card # 3 to the juvenile).
□ Strongly Approve □ Approve □ Disapprove □ Strongly Disapprove

How would your friends respond if they knew you...

1. Used a weapon or force to get money or things from people?
2. Hit someone with the idea of hurting them, for example, fist fighting?

3. Stole something worth $50?
4. Damaged or destroyed someone else's property on purpose?
5. Took a car or motorcycle for a ride without the owner's permission?
6. Used marijuana, reefer, or pot?
7. Used crack?
8. Used heroin?
9. Used cocaine?
10. Used LSD or acid?
11. Carried a gun for protection?

Directions to be read to juvenile. Now, you have thought about people you have hung out with in the past year including your two or three closest friends. I would like to ask you some questions about them during the last year. I am going to read you some activities that kids are sometimes involved in and, think about these friends, then tell me whether None of Them, A Few of them, Some of Them, or All of Them were involved in these activities.

(Provide response card # 4 to the juvenile).
☐ None of Them ☐ A Few of Them ☐ Some of Them ☐ All of Them

In the last year how many of your friends...

12. Drank beer, wine or liquor?
13. Used a weapon or force to get money or things from people?
14. Attacked someone with a weapon or with the idea of seriously hurting them?
15. Hit someone with the idea of hurting them, for example, fist fighting?
16. Stole something worth more than $100?
17. Stole something worth more than $5 but less than $50?
18. Damaged or destroyed someone else's property on purpose?
19. Took a car for a ride without the owner's permission?

(ilecv)
Directions to be read to juvenile. I am going to ask you about things that happened in your neighborhood during the last year. Think about the place(s) that you have lived in the last year and tell me if these things happened Never, Once or Twice, A Few Times, or Many Times.

(Provide response card # 5 to the juvenile).
□ Never □ Once or Twice □ A Few Times □ Many Times

In my neighborhood...

1. I have heard guns being shot.
2. I have seen somebody arrested.
3. I have seen drug deals.
4. I have seen someone being beat up.
5. My house has been broken into.
6. I have seen somebody get stabbed or shot.
7. I have seen gangs in my neighborhood.
8. I have seen somebody pull a gun on another person.
9. I have seen someone in my home get shot or stabbed.

(i1fas)
Directions to be read to juvenile. I am going to ask you some questions about your family. The first few involve some questions about who you live with, then I will ask you some questions about the activities of the parent(s) or guardian that you live with.

1. Who did you live with for the majority of the last calendar year? *(check appropriate box)*
□ Mother only [ask questions in series A and D only, skip series B and C]
□ Father only [ask questions in series B and D only, skip series A and C]
□ Both Mother and Father (includes step-parents) [ask questions in series A, B, and D then skip C]
□ Neither Mother or Father [ask questions in series C and D only, A and B do not apply]

2. Is the person most responsible for you, that is the person considered your primary caretaker or guardian during the last 12 months, male or female?
□ FEMALE □ MALE

Directions for interviewer after juvenile responds to who they lived with:
Below are 4 series of questions, 1 for Mother (SERIES A), 1 for Father (SERIES B), 1 for Guardian, or the person most responsible for the

juvenile's care in the last year (SERIES C) and 1 for how often the youth is involved in family centered activities (SERIES D). Series D should be asked of ALL juveniles, but the other series are conditional based on who the juvenile has lived with for the last year. If the youth identifies himself/herself as living with both mother and father, two series of questions (A and B) should be asked in addition to series D. If the youth identifies only mother or only the father as the person that he or she lived with, then the series for that parent should be filled out as well as series D. If the youth lived with neither parent in any combination for the majority of the last year then only series C, which asks questions about their guardian or caretaker, should be filled out along with Series D.

SERIES A (MOTHER SPECIFIC QUESTIONS) (i1fasm)

1. Is your mother, your biological mother?
   □ YES　　　□ NO

Directions to be read to juvenile. I am going to read you some questions about your Mother. First, I want to ask you about how you relate to your Mother. I am going to read some statements and you tell me if they are Always, Sometimes, Once in a While, or Never true in terms of how you relate to your mother.

(Provide response card # 2 to the juvenile).
□ Never　□ Once in a While　□ Sometimes　□ Always

2. You get along well with your mother…
3. You feel you can really trust your mother…
4. Your mother *does not* understand you…
5. Your mother is too demanding…
6. You really enjoy your mother…
7. You have a lot of respect for your mother…
8. Your mother interferes with your activities…
9. You think your mother is terrific…
10. You feel very angry toward your mother…
11. You feel violent towards your mother…
12. You feel proud of your mother…

Directions to be read to the juvenile. Now I am going to ask you some more questions about how likely you would be to approach your mother about certain things. I will ask you a question and you tell me if you would be Very Likely, Likely, Unlikely, or Very Unlikely to take the action that I am talking about.

(Provide response card # 6 to the juvenile).
□ Very Likely   □ Likely   □ Unlikely   □ Very Unlikely

If you needed to, how likely would you be to...
13. Talk to your mother about personal or private things? Would you say...
14. Ask your mother for advice when you need to make an important decision?
15. Borrow money from your mother?
16. Talk to your mother about problems you are having with your family?
17. Talk to your mother about problems you are having with a friend?
18. Feel you can trust your mother with just about anything you tell her?
19. Talk to your mother about trouble you are having at work or school?
20. Go to your mother for help in an emergency?
21. Go places or do things with your mother?

Directions to be read to the juvenile. Now I am going to ask you some more questions about what your mother knows about your activities. I will ask you a question and you tell me if she Knows Nothing, Knows Just A Little, Knows Some Things, or Knows Everything about the things that I describe.

(Provide response card # 7 to the juvenile).
□ Knows Nothing   □ Knows Very Little   □ Knows Something   □ Knows Everything

22. How much does your mother know about your close friends, that is who they are?
23. How much does your mother know about what you do with your friends?

24. How much does your mother know about your close friends' parents, that is, who they are?

25. How much does your mother know about who you are with when you are not at home?

26. How much does your mother know about who your teachers are?

27. How much does your mother know about what you are doing in school?

Directions to be read to juvenile. I am going to read a couple of statements about your mother. Tell me if you Strongly Disagree, Disagree, Agree, or Strongly Agree with these statements.

(Provide response card # 1 to the juvenile).
□ Strongly Agree □ Agree □ Disagree □ Strongly Disagree

28. I think highly of my mother.
29. My mother is a person I want to be like.
30. I really enjoy spending time with my mother.
31. My mother praises me for doing well.
32. My mother criticizes me and my ideas.
33. My mother helps me do things that are important to me.
34. My mother blames me for her problems.
35. My mother makes plans with me and cancels them for no good reason.

SERIES B (FATHER SPECIFIC QUESTIONS) (i1fasd)

1. Is your father, your biological father?
   □ YES   □ NO

Directions to be read to juvenile. I am going to read you some questions about your Father. First, I want to ask you about how you relate to your Father. I am going to read some statements and you tell me if they are Always, Sometimes, Once in a While, or Never true in terms of how you relate to your father.

(Provide response card # 2 to the juvenile).
□ Never □ Once in a While □ Sometimes □ Always

2. You get along well with your father...

3. You feel you can really trust your father…
4. Your father *does not* understand you…
5. Your father is too demanding…
6. You really enjoy your father…
7. You have a lot of respect for your father…
8. Your father interferes with your activities…
9. You think your father is terrific…
10. You feel very angry toward your father…
11. You feel violent towards your father…
12. You feel proud of your father…

Directions to be read to the juvenile. Now I am going to ask you some more questions about how likely you would be to approach your father about certain things. I will ask you a question and you tell me if you would be Very Likely, Likely, Unlikely, or Very Unlikely to take the action that I am talking about.

(Provide response card # 6 to the juvenile).
□ Very Likely □ Likely □ Unlikely □ Very Unlikely

If you needed to, how likely would you be to…
13. Talk to your father about personal or private things? Would you say…
14. Ask your father for advice when you need to make an important decision?
15. Borrow money from your father?
16. Talk to your father about problems you are having with your family?
17. Talk to your father about problems you are having with a friend?
18. Feel you can trust your father with just about anything you tell him?
19. Talk to your father about trouble you are having at work or school?
20. Go to your father for help in an emergency?
21. Go places or do things with your father?

Directions to be read to the juvenile. Now I am going to ask you some more questions about what your father knows about your activities. I will ask you a question and you tell me if he Knows Nothing, Knows Just A Little, Knows Some Things, or Knows Everything about the things that I describe.

(Provide response card # 7 to the juvenile).

☐ Knows Nothing   ☐ Knows Very Little   ☐ Knows Something   ☐ Knows Everything

22. How much does your father know about your close friends, that is who they are?

23. How much does your father know about what you do with your friends?

24. How much does your father know about your close friends' parents, that is, who they are?

25. How much does your father know about who you are with when you are not at home?

26. How much does your father know about who your teachers are?

27. How much does your father know about what you are doing in school?

Directions to be read to juvenile. I am going to read a couple of statements about your father. Tell me if you Strongly Disagree, Disagree, Agree, or Strongly Agree with these statements.

(Provide response card # 1 to the juvenile).

☐ Strongly Agree   ☐ Agree   ☐ Disagree   ☐ Strongly Disagree

28. I think highly of my father.

29. My father is a person I want to be like.

30. I really enjoy spending time with my father.

31. My father praises me for doing well.

32. My father criticizes me and my ideas.

33. My father helps me do things that are important to me.

34. My father blames me for his problems.

35. My father makes plans with me and cancels them for no good reason.

SERIES C (Guardian SPECIFIC QUESTIONS) (i1fasg)

1. Is the person most responsible for you, that is the person considered your primary caretaker or guardian during the last year, male or female?

☐ FEMALE   ☐ MALE

2. What is that person's first name? _____
2a. What is this person's relationship to you? _____

Substitute that person's name for the blanks in the questions below

Directions to be read to juvenile. I am going to read you some questions about _____. First, I want to ask you about how you relate to _____. I am going to read some statements and you tell me if they are Always, Sometimes, Once in a While, or Never true in terms of how you relate to _____.

(Provide response card # 2 to the juvenile).
□ Never □ Once in a While □ Sometimes □ Always

3. You get along well with _____ ...
4. You feel you can really trust _____ ...
5. _____ *does not* understand you...
6. _____ is too demanding...
7. You really enjoy _____ ...
8. You have a lot of respect for _____ ...
9. _____ interferes with your activities...
10. You think _____ is terrific...
11. You feel very angry toward _____ ...
12. You feel violent toward _____ ...
13. You feel proud of _____ ...

Directions to be read to the juvenile. Now I am going to ask you some more questions about how likely you would be to approach _____ about certain things. I will ask you a question and you tell me if you would be Very Likely, Likely, Unlikely, or Very Unlikely to take the action that I am talking about.

(Provide response card # 6 to the juvenile).
□ Very Likely □ Likely □ Unlikely □ Very Unlikely

If you needed to, how likely would you be to...
14. Talk to _____ about personal or private things? Would you say...
15. Ask _____ for advice when you need to make an important decision?

16. Borrow money from _____?
17. Talk to _____ about problems you are having with your family?
18. Talk to _____ about problems you are having with a friend?
19. Feel you can trust _____ with just about anything you tell him/her?
20. Talk to _____ about trouble you are having at work or school?
21. Go to _____ for help in an emergency?
22. Go places or do things with _____?

Directions to be read to the juvenile. Now I am going to ask you some more questions about what _____ knows about your activities. I will ask you a question and you tell me if she/he Knows Nothing, Knows Just A Little, Knows Some Things, or Knows Everything about the things that I describe.

(Provide response card # 7 to the juvenile).
□ Knows Nothing □ Knows Very Little □ Knows Something □ Knows Everything

23. How much does _____ know about your close friends, that is who they are?
24. How much does _____ know about what you do with your friends?
25. How much does _____ know about your close friends' parents, that is, who they are?
26. How much does _____ know about who you are with when you are not at home?
27. How much does _____ know about who your teachers are?
28. How much does _____ know about what you are doing in school?

Directions to be read to juvenile. I am going to read a couple of statements about _____. Tell me if you Strongly Disagree, Disagree, Agree, or Strongly Agree with these statements.

(Provide response card # 1 to the juvenile).
□ Strongly Agree □ Agree □ Disagree □ Strongly Disagree

29. I think highly of _____ .
30. _____ is a person I want to be like.
31. I really enjoy spending time with _____ .
32. _____ praises me for doing well.
33. _____ criticizes me and my ideas.
34. _____ helps me do things that are important to me.
35. _____ blames me for his/her problems.
36. _____ makes plans with me and cancels them for no good reason.

SERIES D (GENERAL FAMILY QUESTIONS) (i1gfq)

Directions to be read to juvenile. I want you to think about the family that you spent most of your time with in the last year. I am going to ask you some questions about how often you do things with the rest of your family during a normal week. Tell me if you do these things 0, 1, 2, 3, 4, 5, 6, or 7 times a week with your family during a typical week.

Interviewer: Fill in juvenile's response in the space provided.

1. In a typical week, how many days, from 0 to 7, do you eat dinner with your family? _____
2. In a typical week, how many days, from 0 to 7, does housework get done when it is supposed to, for example cleaning up after dinner, doing dishes, or taking out the trash? _____
3. In a typical week, how many days, from 0 to 7, do you do something fun as a family such as play a game, go to a sporting event, go swimming, or some other fun activity? _____
4. In a typical week, how many days, from 0 to 7, do you do something religious as a family such as go to church, pray or read the scriptures together? _____

(i1suls)
Directions to be read to juvenile. I am going to read you a list of things that kids may or may not experience. Think back to the last year and tell me YES if you experienced this or were involved in the activity that I ask about in the last year or NO if you did not.

1. During the last year, did you get poor grades on your report card?
   □ Yes   □ No

2. During the last year, have you gotten into trouble with a teacher or principal at school?

◻ Yes ◻ No

3. During the last year, did you get suspended from school?

◻ Yes ◻ No

4. During the last year, did your family move to a new home or apartment?

◻ Yes ◻ No

5. During the last year, has your family had a new baby come into the family?

◻ Yes ◻ No

6. During the last year, has anyone moved out of your home?

◻ Yes ◻ No

7. During the last year, did a family member die?

◻ Yes ◻ No

8. During the last year, has a family member become seriously ill, injured badly, and/or had to stay at the hospital?

◻ Yes ◻ No

9. During the last year, has someone else you know, other than a member of your family, gotten beaten, attacked or really hurt by others?

◻ Yes ◻ No

10. During the last year, have you seen anyone beaten, shot or really hurt by someone?

◻ Yes ◻ No

11. In the past year, did you change where you go to school?

◻ Yes ◻ No

12. During the last year, have you seen or been around people shooting guns?

◻ Yes ◻ No

13. During the last year, have you had to hide someplace because of shootings in your neighborhood?

◻ Yes ◻ No

Directions to be read to juvenile. As I mentioned at the beginning of this interview, I am from Michigan State University, and am not in any way working for the police, the schools, or any other agency in the city. We are looking to gather information about youth to better understand why they sometimes get into trouble. Your individual information will be kept confidential and will be protected to the maximum extent allowable by law.

(i1abs)
Directions to be read to juvenile. This section asks some questions about situations that you might have been involved in. Think back on the last year and respond to the following questions as completely and accurately as possible. If you had no opportunity to do this, please tell me. If you did, indicate how often you did it in the past year (Never, 1-2 times, 3-4 times, 5 or more times) even if you never did it, but had the opportunity to do it in the last year.

(Provide response card # 8 to the juvenile).
□ No Opportunity □ Never □ 1-2 Times □ 3-4 Times □ 5 + Times

1. I hit back when someone hit me first.
2. I encouraged others to fight.
3. I pushed, shoved, slapped, or kicked others.
4. I got into a physical fight because I was angry.
5. I walked away from a fight.
6. I teased other kids.
7. I said things about other kids to make others laugh (made fun of them).
8. I called other kids names.
9. I threatened to hit or hurt another kid.

(i1fdb)
Directions to be read to juvenile. The following section asks some questions about whether you were *EVER* involved in certain activities that kids sometimes do. Answer YES if you have, and NO if you have not. Then, I will ask you to think back about that activity and the last year and **how many times** you were involved in that activity.

1. Have you ever skipped school without an excuse?
a. □ Yes □ No
b. At what age did you first do this_____?
c. How many times have you done this in the last 12 months___?
2. Have you ever cheated on school tests?
a. □ Yes □ No
b. At what age did you first do this_____?

c. How many times have you done this in the last 12 months___?
3. Have you ever been sent home from school for bad behavior?
a. □ Yes □ No
b. At what age did you first do this_____?
c. How many times have you done this in the last 12 months___?
4. Have you ever run away from home?
a. □ Yes □ No
b. At what age did you first do this_____?
c. How many times have you done this in the last 12 months___?
5. Have you ever, on purpose, broken or damaged or destroyed something belonging to someone else?
a. □ Yes □ No
b. At what age did you first do this_____?
c. How many times have you done this in the last 12 months___?
6. Have you ever taken money at home that did not belong to you like from your mother's purse or your parents' dresser?
a. □ Yes □ No
b. At what age did you first do this_____?
c. How many times have you done this in the last 12 months___?
7. Have you ever gone into somebody's garden, backyard, house, or garage when you were not supposed to be there?
a. □ Yes □ No
b. At what age did you first do this_____?
c. How many times have you done this in the last 12 months___?
8. Have you ever taken anything from a car that did not belong to you?
a. □ Yes □ No
b. At what age did you first do this_____?
c. How many times have you done this in the last 12 months___?
9. Have you ever taken something from a store without paying for it?
a. □ Yes □ No
b. At what age did you first do this_____?
c. How many times have you done this in the last 12 months___?
10. Have you ever thrown rocks or bottles at people?
a. □ Yes □ No
b. At what age did you first do this_____?
c. How many times have you done this in the last 12 months___?
11. Have you ever taken a car or motorcycle for a ride without the owner's permission?
a. □ Yes □ No
b. At what age did you first do this_____?

c. How many times have you done this in the last 12 months___?

12. Have you ever used a weapon or force to get money or things from people?

a. □ Yes □ No

b. At what age did you first do this_____?

c. How many times have you done this in the last 12 months___?

13. Have you ever consumed any liquor?

a. □ Yes □ No

b. At what age did you first do this_____?

c. How many times have you done this in the last 12 months___?

14. Have you ever chewed tobacco?

a. □ Yes □ No

b. At what age did you first do this_____?

c. How many times have you done this in the last 12 months___?

15. Have you ever smoked marijuana?

a. □ Yes □ No

b. At what age did you first do this_____?

c. How many times have you done this in the last 12 months___?

16. Have you ever smoked cigarettes?

a. □ Yes □ No

b. At what age did you first do this_____?

c. How many times have you done this in the last 12 months___?

17. Have you ever sniffed glue?

a. □ Yes □ No

b. At what age did you first do this_____?

c. How many times have you done this in the last 12 months___?

18. Have you ever used cocaine?

a. □ Yes □ No

b. At what age did you first do this_____?

c. How many times have you done this in the last 12 months___?

19. Have you ever abused prescription medications?

a. □ Yes □ No

b. At what age did you first do this_____?

c. How many times have you done this in the last 12 months___?

20. Have you ever used ecstasy?

a. □ Yes □ No

b. At what age did you first do this_____?

c. How many times have you done this in the last 12 months___?

21. Have you ever attended a rave?

a. □ Yes □ No

b. At what age did you first do this_____?

c. How many times have you done this in the last 12 months___?

22. Have you ever used any other types of drugs (besides marijuana)?

a. ☐ Yes ☐ No

b. At what age did you first do this_____?

c. How many times have you done this in the last 12 months___? d. What drugs have you used_____?

23. Have you ever hit, slapped, or shoved a grown-up such as a parent or teacher?

a. ☐ Yes ☐ No

b. At what age did you first do this_____?

c. How many times have you done this in the last 12 months___?

24. Have you ever hit, slapped, or shoved other kids or got into a physical fight with them?

a. ☐ Yes ☐ No

b. At what age did you first do this_____?

c. How many times have you done this in the last 12 months___?

25. Have you ever written things or sprayed paint on walls or sidewalks or cars, where you were not supposed to do that?

a. ☐ Yes ☐ No

b. At what age did you first do this_____?

c. How many times have you done this in the last 12 months___?

26. Have you ever been loud or rowdy in a public place so that people complained about it or you got into trouble?

a. ☐ Yes ☐ No

b. At what age did you first do this_____?

c. How many times have you done this in the last 12 months___?

27. Have you ever purposely set fire to a building, a car, or something else or tried to do so?

a. ☐ Yes ☐ No

b. At what age did you first do this_____?

c. How many times have you done this in the last 12 months___?

28. Have you ever carried a weapon with you?

a. ☐ Yes ☐ No

b. At what age did you first do this_____?

c. How many times have you done this in the last 12 months___?

d. Type of weapon: _____

29. Have you ever avoided paying for things such as movies, bus or subway rides, or food?

a. ☐ Yes ☐ No

b. At what age did you first do this_____?
c. How many times have you done this in the last 12 months___?
30. Have you ever snatched someone's purse or wallet or picked someone's pocket?
a. □ Yes □ No
b. At what age did you first do this_____?
c. How many times have you done this in the last 12 months___?
31. Have you ever been arrested?
a. □ Yes □ No
b. At what age did you first do this_____?
c. How many times have you done this in the last 12 months___?
32. Have you ever gone to court?
a. □ Yes □ No
b. At what age did you first do this_____?
c. How many times have you done this in the last 12 months___?

ASSESSMENT OF THE INTERVIEW
(i1aoi)
This section asks you about your responses to questions in this survey.

1. In your opinion, what causes kids to get in trouble?
Check all that youth mentions

□ Family problems   □ Bad Luck
□ School problems   □ Using alcohol or drugs
□ Being Angry   □ Friends
□ Being Depressed   □ Other_____

Respond with the answer that is, in your opinion, most accurate.

2. While you were answering the interviewer's questions, how accurate were your responses?
□ Very Accurate □ Somewhat Accurate □ Somewhat Inaccurate □ Very Inaccurate
3. While you were answering the interviewer's questions, how truthful were your responses?
□ Very Truthful □ Somewhat Truthful □ Somewhat Untruthful □ Very Untruthful
4. How helpful will these questions be in helping researchers understand why kids get in trouble?

☐ Very Helpful ☐ Somewhat Helpful ☐ Not Helpful at All
5. How helpful will these questions be in understanding why you get in trouble?

☐ Very Helpful ☐ Somewhat Helpful ☐ Not Helpful at All

Interviewer Assessment*

Poor   Fair   Good   Excellent

Interviewers interpretation of how well the interview went. For example, did the youth understand the questions? Did the youth appear attentive? Did the youth appear to put some thought into the answers?

Description of Variables/Measures

Variable	Definition
Outcome Variables	
Official Delinquency	A dichotomous variable with individuals who were arrested within six months following the initial interview (start of program for treatment youth) = 1; not arrested = 0.
Self-reported Violent	A dichotomous variable with youth who self-report violent behavior in the 12 months prior to the first interview (for i1) or the 6 months prior to the second interview (for i2) = 1; no violent behavior reported = 0. Violent behaviors included: assaulting a peer, assaulting an adult, and thrown rocks or bottles at people.
Self-reported Nonviolent	A dichotomous variable with youth who self-report nonviolent behavior in the 12 months prior to the first interview (for i1) or the 6 months prior to the second interview (for i2) = 1; no nonviolent behavior reported = 0. Nonviolent behaviors included: malicious destruction of property, theft from parents, trespassing, theft from car, shoplifting, graffiti, arson, and auto theft.
Self-reported Drug Use	A dichotomous variable with youth who self-report substance using in the 12 months prior to the first interview (for i1) or the 6 months prior to the second interview (for i2) = 1; no substance use reported = 0. Substance use included: consumed any liquor, smoked marijuana, smoked cigarettes, and used cocaine.
Self-reported Variety	A variable that represents the number of unique delinquent behaviors the youth reported in the 12 months prior to the first interview. Eighteen separate behaviors were divided into two separate (but statistically equivalent) parallel scores representing variety of self-reported general delinquency. Behaviors included: skipped school, cheated on school test, sent home from school for bad behavior, run away from home, destruction of property, theft from parents, theft from car, trespassing, shoplifting, thrown rocks or bottles at people, consumed liquor, smoked marijuana, smoked cigarettes, assault adult, assault peer, graffiti, disorderly conduct, and carried a weapon. See the chapter 3 (or Lyons, Zarit, Sayer, & Whitlatch, 2002; Coley & Morris, 2002) for a

more thorough discussion of parallel scores. This
variable was only used for the HLM analysis.

Variable	Definition
Explanatory Variables	
Family Bond (mean)	A mean score ($\alpha=0.875$) including the following 10 questions: (1) "I feel I can really trust my primary caretaker;" (2) "I really enjoy my primary caretaker;" (3) "I think my primary caretaker is terrific;" (4) "I feel proud of my primary caretaker;" (5) "I feel I can trust my primary caretaker with just about anything I tell him/her;" (6) "I talk to my primary caretaker about trouble I am having at work or school;" (7) "I go places or do things with my primary caretaker;" (8) "I think highly of my primary caretaker;" (9) "my primary caretaker is a person I want to be like;" and (10) "I really enjoy spending time with my primary caretaker." Response set for items 1-4 was "never," "once in a while," "sometimes," and "always." For items 5-7, the response set was "very likely," "likely," "unlikely," and "very unlikely." Finally, the response set for items 8-10 was "strongly agree," "agree," "disagree," and "strongly disagree."
Family Bond (change)	A change score representing the difference in mean family bond from interview 1 (i1) to interview 2 (i2).
Family Programming	Number of minutes of family counseling or other family oriented programming treatment youth received while in the program.
Single Parent Family	A dichotomous variable with youth residing in a single parent family = 1; youth with two parents in household (biological parents or step parents) = 0.
Days in Program	Number of days the treatment youth were in the program prior to the first interview.
White	A dichotomous variable with white = 1; African American, Hispanic, or other race = 0.
Age	Juvenile's age measured in years.
Male	A dichotomous variable with males = 1; female = 0.

APPENDIX C
Correlation Matrices

Table C1. Correlation Matrix (Treatment Group; N = 68)

		X_2	X_3	X_4	X_5	X_6	X_7	X_8	X_9	Y_1	Y_2	Y_3	Y_4
X_1	White	-.049	.002	.091	-.358*	.047	-.078	-.071	.010	-.159	-.019	.121	-.131
X_2	Male	--	-.027	.127	.240*	.008	.070	.124	.052	.080	.136	.086	-.039
X_3	Age		--	-.151	-.077	-.300*	.024	-.039	-.064	.145	.067	.249*	.266*
X_4	Days in Program			--	-.041	-.140	-.089	.102	.197	-.211	-.045	.323*	.211
X_5	Single Parent Family				--	-.051	-.048	.173	.225	-.088	-.103	.051	-.102
X_6	Family Prog. Minutes					--	.175	-.047	-.230	.143	.181	-.104	-.149
X_7	Family Bond i1 (mean)						--	.528*	-.511*	-.026	.020	-.062	-.041
X_8	Family Bond i2 (mean)							--	.460*	-.190	-.300*	-.079	-.037
X_9	Family Bond Change								--	-.165	-.324*	-.015	.005
Y_1	Prev. Score – Violent									--	.367*	.236	.038
Y_2	Prev. Score – Nonviolent										--	.382*	-.027
Y_3	Prev. Score – Drug											--	.162
Y_4	6 month failure												--

*p < .05 (two-tailed test)

156

Table C2. Correlation Matrix (Comparison Group; N = 83)

		X_2	X_3	X_4	X_5	X_6	X_7	X_8	X_9	Y_1	Y_2	Y_3
X_1	White	-.382*	.341*	--	-.187	--	.183	.039	-.166	.097	.216	.100
X_2	Male	--	-.129	--	-.016	--	-.134	-.140	-.021	.123	-.111	.220*
X_3	Age		--	--	.132	--	-.161	-.097	.066	.150	.172	.286*
X_4	Days in Program			--	--	--	--	--	--	--	--	--
X_5	Single Parent Family				--	--	-.292*	-.253*	.022	.017	.077	-.055
X_6	Family Programming Minutes					--	--	--	--	--	--	--
X_7	Family Bond i1 (mean)						--	.673*	-.321*	-.178	-.268*	-.072
X_8	Family Bond i2 (mean)							--	.485*	-.328*	-.366*	-.228*
X_9	Family Bond Change								--	-.210	-.151	-.207
Y_1	Prevalence Score – Violent									--	.432*	.577*
Y_2	Prevalence Score – Nonviolent										--	.472*
Y_3	Prevalence Score – Drug											--

*$p < .05$ (two-tailed test)

City and Target Area Characteristics

Table D1. Descriptive Statistics for the City and Target Area

	City	Target Area
Total population	207,886	51,734
Percent male	48.92	50.54
Percent minority	31.56	29.24
Percent foreign born	10.35	16.29
Percent renter occupied units	37.87	38.22
Percent of families with children split	19.39	22.87
Percent of individuals with college education (over 25 years old)	24.66	13.71
Percent of families with income greater than $25,000	68.45	65.91
Percent of families below the poverty level	11.47	13.06
Percent of households receiving public assistance	4.71	5.60
Percent female headed households	23.73	25.69
Percent unemployed (over 16 and in labor force)	6.11	7.60
Percent youth	26.79	29.48
Percent African-American	19.30	10.34
Percent of buildings that are vacant	6.11	7.09
Concentrated disadvantage*	-0.004	0.011

*Factor Score – higher values indicate more disadvantage

Bibliography

Agnew, R. (1992). Foundation for a general strain theory of crime and delinquency. *Criminology, 30*(1), 47-87.

Agnew, R. (2005). *Why Do Criminals Offend? A General Theory of Crime and Delinquency.* Los Angeles: Roxbury.

Akers, R. (1985). *Deviant Behavior: A Social Learning Approach* (3rd ed.). Belmont, CA, Wadsworth.

Akers, R. (1991). Self-control as a general theory of crime. *Journal of Quantitative Criminology, 7*(2), 201-211.

Akers, R. L. (1998). *Social Learning and Social Structure: A General Theory of Crime and Deviance.* Boston: Northeastern University Press.

Akers, R. L. (2000). *Criminological Theories.* Los Angeles: Roxbury.

Alarid, L. F., Burton, Jr., V. S., Cullen, F. T. (2000). Gender and crime among felony offenders: Assessing the generality of social control and differential association theories. *Journal of Research in Crime and Delinquency, 37*(2), 171-199.

Alexander, J., Barton, C., Gordon, D., Grotpeter, J., Hansson, K., Harrison, R., Mears, S., Mihalic, S., Parsons, B., Pugh, C., Schulman, S., Waldron, H., & Sexton, T. (1998). *Blueprints for Violence Prevention, Book Three: Functional Family Therapy.* Boulder, CO: Center for the Study and Prevention of Violence.

Anderson, A. L. (2002). Individual and contextual influences on delinquency: The role of the single-parent family. *Journal of Criminal Justice, 30*(6), 575-587.

Anderson, B. J., Holmes, M. D., Ostresh, E. (1999). Male and female delinquents' attachments and effects of attachments on severity of self-reported delinquency. *Criminal Justice and Behavior, 26*(4), 435-452.

Andrews, D. A., Zinger, I., Hoge, R. D., Bonta, J., Gendreau, P., & Cullen, F. T. (1990). Does correctional treatment work? A clinically-relevant and psychologically-informed meta-analysis. *Criminology, 28*(3), 369-404.

Ayers, C. D., Williams, J. H., Hawkins, J. D., Peterson, P. L., Catalano, R. F., & Abbott, R. D. (1999). Assessing correlates of onset, escalation, de-escalation, and desistance of delinquent behavior. *Journal of Quantitative Criminology, 15*(3), 277-306.

Bandura, A. (1973). *Aggression: A Social Learning Analysis.* Englewood Cliffs, N.J.: Prentice-Hall.

Bandura, A. (1986). *Social Foundations of Thought and Action.* New York: Prentice Hall.

Bank, L. & Burraston, B. (2001). Abusive home environments as predictors of poor adjustment during adolescence and early adulthood. *Journal of Community Psychology, 29*(3), 195-217.

Beccaria, C. (1963). *On Crimes and Punishments,* translated by Henry Paolucci, Indianapolis: Bobbs-Merrill.

Besharov, D. J. (1987). Giving the juvenile court a preschool education. In J. Q. Wilson & G. C. Loury (eds.). *From Children to Citizens (Vol III): Families, Schools, and Delinquency Prevention* (pp. 207-238). New York: Springer-Verlag.

Black, M. M, Howard, D. E., Kim, N., & Ricardo, I. (1998). Interventions to prevent violence among African American Adolescents from low-income communities. *Aggression and Violent Behavior, 3*(1), 17-33.

Blumstein, A., Cohen, J., Roth, J. A., & Visher, C. A. (1986). *Criminal Careers and Career Criminals.* Washington DC: National Academy Press.

Borduin, C. M. (1994). Innovative models of treatment and service delivery in the juvenile justice system. *Journal of Clinical Child Psychology, 23,* 19-26.

Borduin, C. M., Cone, L. T., Mann, B. J., Henggeler, S. W., Fucci, B. R., Blaske, D. M., & Williams, R. A. (1995). Multisystemic treatment of serious juvenile offenders: Long-term prevention of criminality and violence. *Journal of Consulting and Clinical Psychology, 63,* 569-578.

Bowbly, J. (1947). *Forty-Four Juvenile Thieves.* London: Bailliero, Tindall, and Cox.

Bowen, M. (1978). *Family Therapy in Clinical Practice.* Northvale, NJ: Jason Aronson.

Bray J. H. & Hetherington, E. M. (1993). Families in transition: Introduction and overview. *Journal of Family Psychology, 7*(1), 3-8.

Brooks-Gunn, J., Duncan, G. J., Klebanov, P. K., & Sealand, N. (1993). Do neighborhoods influence child and adolescent development? *American Journal of Sociology, 99*(2), 353-395.

Bronfrenbrenner, U. (1979). *The Ecology of Human Development: Experiments by Design and Nature.* Cambridge, MA: Harvard University Press.

Browning, K., Huizinga, D., Loeber, R., & Thornberry, T. P. (1999). *Fact Sheet: Causes and Correlates of Delinquency Program.* Washington, D.C.: Office of Juvenile Justice and Delinquency Prevention.

Burgess, R. & Akers, R. (1966). A differential association-reinforcement theory of criminal behavior. *Social Problems, 14,* 128-147.

Burns, B. J., Howell, J. C., Wiig, J. K., Augimeri, L. K., Welsh, B. C., Loeber, R. et al., (2003). *Treatment, Services, and Intervention Programs for Child Delinquents.* Washington DC: Office of Juvenile Justice and Delinquency Prevention.

Bursik, R. J. Jr. (1988). Social disorganization and theories of crime and delinquency: Problems and prospects. *Criminology, 26,* 519-551.

Burton, V. S. Jr., Cullen, F. T., Evans, D., Alarid, L F., & Dunaway, R. G. (1998). Gender, self-control, and crime. *Journal of Research in Crime and Delinquency, 35,* 123-147.

Cantor, R. J. (1982). Family correlates of male and female delinquency. *Criminology, 20,* 149-166.

Caspi, A., Moffitt, T. E., Silva, P. A., Loeber, M. S., Krueger, R. F., & Schmutte, P. S. (1994). Are some people crime-prone? Replications of the personality-crime relationship across countries, genders, races, and methods. *Criminology, 32,* 163-196.

Catalano, R. F. & Hawkins, J. D. (1996). The social development model: A theory of antisocial behavior. In J. D. Hawkins (ed.). *Delinquency and Crime: Current Theories* (pp. 149-197). Cabridge, UK: Cambridge University Press.

Cernkovich, S. A. (1978). Evaluating two models of delinquency causation. *Criminology, 16*(3), 335-354.

Cernkovich, S. A. & Giordano, P. C. (1987). Family Relationships and Delinquency. *Criminology 25*(2), 295-321.

Cernkovich, S.A. & Giordano, P. C. (1992). School bonding, race, and delinquency. *Criminology, 30*(2), 261-289.

Cobb, N. J. (2001). *Adolescence.* Mountain View, CA: Mayfield Publishing Company.

Coleman, J. S. (1988). Social capital in the creation of human capital. *American Journal of Sociology, 94*, S95-120.

Coley, R. L. & Morris, J. E. (2002). Comparing father and mother reports of father involvement among low-income minority families. *Journal of Marriage and Family, 64*(4), 982-995.

Connell, A. M. & Goodman, S. H. (2002). The association between psychopathology in fathers versus mothers and children's internalizing and externalizing behavior problems: A meta-analysis. *Psychological Bulletin, 128*(5), 746-773.

Costello, B. J. & Vowell, P. R. (1999). Testing control theory and differential association. *Criminology, 37*(4), 815-42.

Cullen, F. T. (2005). The twelve people who saved rehabilitation: How the science of criminology made a difference. The American Society of Criminology 2004 presidential address. *Criminology, 43*(1), 1-42.

Cullen, F. T., Wright, J. P., Brown, S., Moon, M. M., Blankenship, M. B., & Applegate, B. K. (1998). Public support for early intervention programs: Implications for a progressive policy agenda. *Crime & Delinquency, 44*(2), 187-204.

Davies, M. & Sinclair, I. (1971). Families, hostels and delinquents: An attempt to assess cause and effect. *British Journal of Criminology, 11*(3), 213-229.

Demuth, S. & Brown, S. L. (2004). Family structure, family processes, and adolescent delinquency: The significance of parental absence versus parental gender. *Journal of Research in Crime and Delinquency, 41*(1), 58-81.

Dishion, T. J., French, D. C., & Patterson, G. R. (1999). Middle childhood antecedents to the progressions in male adolescent substance use: An ecological analysis of risk and protection. *Journal of Adolescent Research, 14*(2), 175-205.

Dornbusch, S. M., Erickson, K. G., Laird, J., Wong, C. A. (2001). The relation of family and school attachment to adolescent deviance in diverse groups and communities. *Journal of Adolescent Research, 16*(4), 396-422.

Dowden, C. & Andrews, D. A. (2003). Does family intervention work for delinquents? Results of a meta-analysis. *Canadian Journal of Criminology and Criminal Justice, 45*(3), 327-342.

Durkheim, E. (1951). *Suicide*. New York: Free Press.

Eamon, M. K. & Venkataraman, M. (2003). Implementing parent management training in the context of poverty. *The American Journal of Family Therapy, 31*, 281-293.

Elliott, D. S. (1994). Serious violent offenders: Onset, developmental course, and termination: The American Society of Criminology 1993 presidential address. *Criminology, 32*, 1-21.

Elliott, D. S. & Ageton, S. S. (1980). Reconciling race and class differences in self-reported and official estimates of delinquency. *American Sociological Review, 45*, 95-110.

Elliott, D. S., Huizinga, D., & Ageton, S. S. (1985). *Explaining Delinquency and Drug Use*. Beverly Hills, CA: Sage.

Erickson, K. G., Crosnoe, R., Dornbusch, S. M. (2000). A social process model of adolescent deviance: Combining social control and differential association perspectives. *Journal of Youth and Adolescence, 29*(4), 395-425.

Espiritu, R. C., Huizinga, D., Crawford, A. M., & Loeber, R. (2001). Epidemiology of self-reported delinquency. In R. Loeber & D. P. Farrington (Eds.). *Child Delinquents: Development, Intervention, and Service Needs* (pp. 47-66). Thousand Oaks, CA: Sage.

Fagan, J.A. and Wexler. S. (1987). Family origins of violent delinquents. *Criminology 25*(3), 643-669.

Farrington, D. P. (1986). Age and crime. In M. Tonry and N. Morris (Eds.). *Crime and Justice: An Annual Review of Research* (Vol. 7, pp 189-250). Chicago: University of Chicago Press.

Farrington, D. P. (1987). Early precursors of frequent offending. In J. Q. Wilson and G. C. Loury (Eds.), *From Children to Citizens (Vol III): Families, Schools, and Delinquency Prevention* (pp. 27-50). New York: Springer-Verlag.

Farrington, D. P. (1995). The development of offending and antisocial behavior from childhood: Key findings from the Cambridge study in delinquent development. *Journal of Child Psychology and Psychiatry, 36*(1), 1-36

Farrington, D. P. & Loeber, R. (1998). Major aims of this book. In R. Loeber & D. P. Farrington (Eds.), *Serious & Violent Juvenile*

Offenders: Risk Factors and Successful Interventions (pp. 1-12). Thousand Oaks: Sage.

Fields, J. & Casper, L. M. (2001). America's families and living arrangements: March 2000. Current Population Reports, P20-537. U.S. Census Bureau, Washington, DC.

Fleming, C. B., Catalano, R. F., Oxford, M. L., & Harachi, T. W. (2002). A test of generalizability of the social development model across gender and income groups with longitudinal data from the elementary school development period. *Journal of Quantitative Criminology, 18*(4), 423-439.

Fox, J. (1991). *Regression Diagnostics*. Thousand Oaks, CA: Sage.

Gavazzi, S. M., Yarcheck, C. M., Rhine, E. E., & Partridge, C. R. (2003). Building bridges between the parole officer and the families of serious juvenile offenders: A preliminary report on a family-based parole program. *International Journal of Offender Therapy and Comparative Criminology, 47*(3), 291-308.

Geis, G. (2000). On the absence of self-control as the basis for a general theory of crime. *Theoretical Criminology, 4*, 35-53.

Gerard, J. M. & Buehler, C. (1999). Multiple risk factors in the family environment and youth problem behaviors. *Journal of Marriage and the Family, 61*, 343-361.

Gibbons, D. C. (1999). Review essay: Changing lawbreakers—what have we learned since the 1950's? *Crime and Delinquency, 45*, 272-293.

Glueck, S. & Glueck, E. T. (1950). *Unraveling Juvenile Delinquency*. New York: Commonwealth Fund.

Glueck, S. & Glueck, E. T. (1952). *Delinquents in the Making: Paths to Prevention*. New York: Harper and Row.

Glueck, S. & Glueck, E. T. (1962). *Family Environment and Delinquency*. Boston: Houghton Mifflin.

Goldstein, J. R. (1999). The leveling of divorce in the United States. *Demography, 36*(3), 409-414.

Gordon, D. A., Graves, K., & Arbuthnot, J. (1995). The effect of functional family therapy for delinquents on adult criminal behavioral. *Criminal Justice Behavior, 22*, 60-73.

Gordon, D. A., Arbuthnot, J., Gustafson, K. A., & McGreen, P. (1988). Home-based behavioral-systems family therapy with disadvantaged juvenile delinquents. *American Journal of Family Therapy, 16*(3), 243-255.

Gorman-Smith, D., Tolan, P. H., Zelli, A., & Huesmann, L. R. (1996). The relation of family functioning to violence among inner-city youth. *Journal of Family Psychology, 10*(2), 115-129.

Gorman-Smith, D., Tolan, P. H., Loeber, R., & Henry, D. B. (1998). Relation of family problems to patterns of delinquent involvement among urban youth. *Journal of Abnormal Child Psychology, 26*(5), 319-333.

Gottfredson, M. R. & Hirschi, T. (1987). The methodological adequacy of longitudinal research on crime. *Criminology 25*, 581-614.

Gottfredson, M. R. & Hirschi, T. (1990). *A General Theory of Crime.* Stanford, CA: Stanford University Press.

Grasmick, H. G., Tittle, C. R., Bursik, Jr. R. J., & Arneklev, B. J. (1993). Testing the core empirical implications of Gottfredson and Hirschi's general theory of crime. *Journal of Research in Crime and Delinquency, 30*(1), 5-29.

Greenberg, D. F. (1999). The weak strength of social control theory. *Crime and Delinquency, 45*, 66-81.

Greenberg, D. F. (1985). Age, crime, and social explanation. *American Journal of Sociology, 91*(1), 1-21.

Guerra, N. G. (1998). Serious and violent juvenile offenders: Gaps in knowledge and research priorities. In R. Loeber & D. P. Farrington (Eds.), *Serious & Violent Juvenile Offenders: Risk Factors and Successful Interventions* (pp. 389-404). Thousand Oaks: Sage.

Haas, H., Farrington, D. P., Killias, M., & Sattar, G. (2004). The impact of different family configurations on delinquency. *British Journal of Criminology, 44*(4), 520-532.

Hawkins, J. D., Catalano, R. F., Jones, G., & Fine, D. (1987). Delinquency prevention through parent training: Results and Issues from work in progress. In J. Q. Wilson and G. C. Loury (Eds.), *From Children to Citizens (Vol III): Families, Schools, and Delinquency Prevention* (pp. 186-204). New York: Springer-Verlag.

Hawkins, D. F., Laub, J. H., & Lauritsen, J. L. (1998). Race, ethnicity, and serious juvenile offending. In R. Loeber & D. P. Farrington (Eds.), *Serious & Violent Juvenile Offenders: Risk Factors and Successful Interventions* (pp. 30-46). Thousand Oaks: Sage.

Hay, C. (2001). Parenting, self-control, and delinquency: A test of self-control theory. *Criminology, 39*(3), 707-736.

Heck, C. & Walsh, A. (2000). The effects of maltreatment and minor and serious delinquency. *International Journal of Offender Therapy and Comparative Criminology, 44*(2), 178-193.

Henggeler, S. W. (1996). Treatment of violent juvenile offenders—We have the knowledge: Comment on Gorman-Smith et al. (1996). *Journal of Family Psychology, 10*(2), 137-141.

Henggeler, S. W. (1997). *Treating Serious Antisocial Behavior in Youth: The MST Approach.* Washington DC: Office of Juvenile Justice and Delinquency Prevention.

Henggeler, S. W., Melton, G. B., & Smith, L. A. (1992). Family preservation using multisystemic therapy: An effective alternative to incarcerating serious juvenile offenders. *Journal of Consulting and Clinical Psychology, 60*(6), 953-961.

Herrenkohl, T. I, Hawkins, J. D., Chung, I-J., Hill, K. G., & Battin-Pearson, S. (2001). School and community risk factors and interventions. In R. Loeber & D. P. Farrington (Eds.), *Child Delinquents: Development, Intervention, and Service Needs* (pp. 211-246). Thousand Oaks, CA: Sage.

Herrenkohl, T. I., Huang, B., Kosterman, R., Hawkins, J. D., Catalano, R. F., & Smith, B. H. (2001). A comparison of social development processes leading to violent behavior in late adolescence for childhood initiators and adolescent initiators of violence. *Journal of Research in Crime and Delinquency, 38*(1), 45-63.

Hill, K. G., Howell, J. C., Hawkins, J. D., & Battin-Pearson, S. R. (1999). Childhood risk factors for adolescent gang membership: Results from the Seattle social development project. *Journal of Research in Crime and Delinquency, 36*(3), 300-322.

Hindelang, M. J., Hirschi, T., & Weis, J. G. (1981). *Measuring Delinquency.* Beverly Hills, CA: Sage.

Hirschi, T. (1969). *Causes of Delinquency.* Berkley: University of California Press.

Hirschi, T., & Gottfredson, M. (1983). Age and the explanation of crime. *American Journal of Sociology, 89*, 552-584.

Ho, T. P., Chow, V., & Fung, C. (1999). Parent management training in a Chinese population: Application and outcome. *Journal of the American Academy of Child and Adolescent Psychiatry, 38*(9), 1165-72.

Howell, J. C. (1995). *Guide for Implementing the Comprehensive Strategy for Serious, Violent, and Chronic Juvenile Offenders.*

Washington, DC: Office of Juvenile Justice and Delinquency Prevention.

Huang, B., Klosterman, R., Catalano, R. F., Hawkins, J.D., & Abbott, R. D. (2001). Modeling mediation in the etiology of violent behavior in adolescence: A test of the social development model. *Criminology, 39*(1), 75-107.

Huizinga, D. & Jakob-Chien, C. (1998). The contemporaneous co-occurrence of serious and violent juvenile offending and other problem behaviors. In R. Loeber & D. P. Farrington (Eds.), *Serious & Violent Juvenile Offenders: Risk Factors and Successful Interventions* (pp. 47-67). Thousand Oaks, CA: Sage.

Hunner, R. & Walker, Y. (Eds.). (1981). *Exploring the Relationship Between Child Abuse and Delinquency.* Montclair, NJ: Allanheld & Schram.

Ingram, J. R., Patchin, J. W., Huebner, B. M., McCluskey, J. D., & Bynum, T. S. (2006). Family Life, Peer Associations, and Serious Delinquency: A Path Analysis. Unpublished paper, Michigan State University.

Ireland, T. O., Smith, C. A., & Thornberry, T. P. (2002). Developmental issues in the impact of child maltreatment on later delinquency and drug use. *Criminology 40*(2), 359-399.

Johnson, R. E. (1986). Family structure and delinquency: General patterns and gender differences. *Criminology, 24*(1), 65-80.

Johnson, R. E. (1987). Mother's versus father's role in causing delinquency. *Adolescence, 22*(86), 305-15.

Jonson, M. R. (1998). Youth violent behavior and exposure to violence in childhood: An ecological review. *Aggression and Violent Behavior, 3*(2), 159-179.

Juby, H. & Farrington, D. P. (2001). Disentangling the link between disrupted families and delinquency. *British Journal of Criminology, 41*(1), 22-40.

Junger, M. & Marshall, I. H. (1997). The interethnic generalizability of social control theory: An empirical test. *Journal of Research in Crime and Delinquency, 34*(1), 79-112.

Junger, M. & Tremblay, R. E. (1999). Self-control, accidents, and crime. *Criminal Justice and Behavior. 26*, 485-501.

Kaplan, S. J., Pelcovitz, D., & Labruna, V. (1999). Child and adolescent abuse and neglect research: A review of the past 10 years. Part I: Physical and emotional abuse and neglect. *Journal* of the American Academy of Child & Adolescent Psychiatry, *38*(10), 1214-1222.

Kazdin, A. E. (1987). Treatment of antisocial behavior in children: Current status and future directions. *Psychological Bulletin, 102,* 187-203.

Kazdin, A. E. (1997). Parent management training: Evidence, outcomes, and issues. *Journal of the American Academy of Child & Adolescent Psychiatry, 36*(10), 1349-1356.

Kazdin, A. E. (2005). *Parent Management Training: Treatment for Oppositional, Aggressive, and Antisocial Behavior in Children and Adolescents.* New York: Oxford University Press.

Kazdin, A. E., Siegel, T. C., & Bass, D. (1992). Cognitive problem-solving skills training and parent management training in the treatment of antisocial behavior in children. *Journal of Consulting and Clinical Psychology, 60*(5), 733-747.

Kempf, K. L. (1993). The empirical status of Hirschi's control theory. In F. Adler and W. S. Laufer (eds.), *New Directions in Criminological Theory: Advances in Criminological Theory* (Vol. 4). New Brunswick, NJ: Transaction.

Kierkus, C. A. & Baer, D. (2003). Does the relationship between family structure and delinquency vary according to circumstances? An investigation of interaction effects. *Canadian Journal of Criminology and Criminal Justice, 45*(4), 405-429.

Knutson, J. F. (1995). Psychological characteristics of maltreated children: Putative risk factors and consequences. *Annual Review of Psychology, 46,* 401-431.

Kornhauser, R. (1978). *Social Sources of Delinquency.* Chicago: University of Chicago Press.

Krohn, M. D. & Massey, J. L. (1980). Social control and delinquent behavior: An examination of the elements of the social bond. *The Sociological Quarterly, 21,* 529-543.

LaGrange, T. C. & Silverman, R. A. (1999). Low self-control and opportunity: Testing the general theory of crime as an explanation for gender differences in delinquency. *Criminology, 37*(1), 41-72.

Latimer, J. (2001). A meta-analytic examination of youth delinquency, family treatment, and recidivism. *Canadian Journal of Criminology, 43,* 237-253.

Laub, J. H. & Sampson, R. J. (1991). The Sutherland-Glueck debate: On the sociology of criminological knowledge. *American Journal of Sociology, 96,* 1402-1440.

Lipsey, M. W. (1999). Can intervention rehabilitate serious delinquents? *Annals of the American Association of Political and Social Science, 564*, 142-166.

Lipsey, M. W. & Derzon, J.H. (1998). Predictors of violent or serious delinquency in adolescence and early adulthood: A synthesis of longitudinal research. In R. Loeber & D. P. Farrington (Eds.), *Serious & Violent Juvenile Offenders: Risk Factors and Successful Interventions* (pp. 106-146). Thousand Oaks, CA: Sage.

Lipsey, M. W. & Wilson, D. B. (1998). Effective intervention for serious juvenile offenders: A synthesis of research. In R. Loeber & D. P. Farrington (Eds.), *Serious & Violent Juvenile Offenders: Risk Factors and Successful Interventions* (pp. 313-345). Thousand Oaks, CA: Sage.

Loeber, R. (1982). The stability of antisocial and delinquent child behavior: A review. *Child Development, 53*, 1431-1446.

Loeber, R. (1987). What policy makers and practitioners can learn from family studies of juvenile conduct problems and delinquency. In J. Q. Wilson and G. C. Loury (Eds.), *From Children to Citizens (Vol III): Families, Schools, and Delinquency Prevention* (pp. 78-111). New York: Springer-Verlag.

Loeber, R. & Farrington, D. P. (Eds.). (1998). *Serious & Violent Juvenile Offenders: Risk Factors and Successful Interventions.* Thousand Oaks: Sage. Thousand Oaks, CA: Sage.

Loeber, R. & Farrington, D. P. (Eds.). (2001). *Child Delinquents: Development, Intervention, and Service Needs.* Thousand Oaks, CA: Sage.

Loeber, R., Farrington, D. P., & Waschbusch, D. A. (1998). Serious and violent juvenile offenders. In R. Loeber & D. P. Farrington (Eds.), *Serious & Violent Juvenile Offenders: Risk Factors and Successful Interventions* (pp. 13-29). Thousand Oaks, CA: Sage.

Loeber, R. & Stouthamer-Loeber, M. (1986). Family factors as correlates and predictors of juvenile conduct problems and delinquency. In M. Tonry & N. Morris (Eds.), *Crime and Justice* (pp. 29-149). Chicago: University of Chicago Press.

Loury, G. (1987). The family as context for delinquency prevention: Demographic trends and political realities. In J. Q. Wilson and G. C. Loury (Eds.), *From Children to Citizens (Vol III): Families, Schools, and Delinquency Prevention* (pp. 3-26). New York: Springer-Verlag.

Lynskey, D. P., Winfree, Jr., L. T., Esbensen, F., & Clason, D. L. (2000). Linking gender, minority group status and family matters to self-control theory: A multivariate analysis of key self-control concepts in a youth-gang context. *Juvenile & Family Court Journal, 51*(3), 1-19.

Lyons, K. S., Zarit, S. H., Sayer, A. G., & Whitlatch, C. J. (2002). Caregiving as a dyadic process: Perspectives from caregiver and receiver. Journal of Gerontology, 57B(3), 195-204.

Marcus, B. (2004). Self-control in the general theory of crime: Theoretical implications of a measurement problem. *Theoretical Criminology, 8*(1), 33-55.

Marsh, H. W. & Hau, K. (1999). Confirmatory factor analysis: Strategies for small sample sizes. In R. H. Hoyle (Ed.), *Statistical Strategies for Small Sample Research* (pp. 251-284). Thousand Oaks, CA: Sage.

Martinez, Jr., C. R. & Eddy, J. M. (2005). Effects of culturally adapted parent management training on Latino youth behavioral health outcomes. *Journal of Consulting and Clinical Psychology, 73*(4), 841-851.

Martinson, R. (1974). What works? Questions and answers about prison reform. *Public Interest, 35*, 22-54.

Martinson, R. (1979). Symposium on sentencing: Part II. *Hofstra Law Review, 7*(2), 243-258.

Matsueda, R. L. (1982). Testing control theory and differential association: A causal modeling approach. *American Sociological Review, 47*, 489-504.

Matsueda, R. (1988). The current state of differential association theory. *Crime and Delinquency, 34*, 277-306.

Maxfield, M. G., Weiler, B. L., & Widom, C. S. (2000). Comparing self-reports and official records of arrest. *Journal of Quantitative Criminology, 16*, 87-110.

May, D. C., Vartanian, L. R., & Virgo, K. (2002). The impact of parental attachment and supervision on fear of crime among adolescent males. *Adolescence, 37*(146), 267-287.

Mazerolle, P., Brame, R., Paternoster, R., Piquero, A., & Dean, C. (2000). Onset age, persistence, and offending versatility: Comparisons across gender. *Criminology, 38*(4), 1143-1172.

McCarthy, E. D., Gersten, J. C. & Langner, T. S. (1982). The behavioral effects of father absence on children and their mothers. *Social Behavior and Personality 10*, 11-23.

McCord, J. (1989). A forty year perspective on effects of child abuse and neglect. *Child Abuse & Neglect, 7,* 265-270.

McCord, J. (1991). Family relationships, juvenile delinquency, and adult criminality. *Criminology, 29*(2): 243-266.

Mednick, S. & Christiansen, K. O. (1977). *Biosocial Bases or Criminal Behavior.* New York: Gardner Press.

Menard, S. (1991). *Longitudinal Research.* Thousand Oaks, CA: Sage.

Menard, S. (1995). *Applied Logistic Regression Analysis.* Thousand Oaks, CA: Sage.

Mihalic, S., Irwin, K., Elliott, D., Fagan, A., & Hansen, D. (2001). *Blueprints for Violence Prevention.* Washington DC: Office of Juvenile Justice and Delinquency Prevention.

Miller, K. S. & Knutson, J. F. (1997). Reports of severe physical punishment and exposure to animal cruelty by inmates convicted of felonies and by university students. *Child Abuse & Neglect, 21,* 59-82.

Moffitt, T. E. (1993). Adolescence-limited and life-course persistent antisocial behavior: A developmental taxonomy. *Psychological Review, 100,* 674-701.

Moon, M. M., Sundt, J. L., Cullen, F. T., & Wright, J. P. (2000). Is child saving dead? Public support for juvenile rehabilitation. *Crime & Delinquency, 46*(1), 38-60.

Mullis, R. L., Mullis, A. K., Cornille, T. A., Kershaw, M. A., Beckerman, A., & Perkins, D. (2005). Young chronic offenders: A case study of contextual and intervention characteristics. *Youth Violence and Juvenile Justice, 3*(2), 133-150.

Murray, J. & Farrington, D.P. (2005). Parental imprisonment: Effects on boys' anti-social behaviour and delinquency through the life-course. *Journal of Child Psychology and Psychiatry and Allied Disciplines, 46*(12), 1269-1278.

Nagin, D. & Paternoster, R. (1991). On the relationship of past and future participation in delinquency. *Criminology, 29,* 163-190.

Needle, R., Su, S., Doherty, W., Lavee, Y., & Brown, P. (1988). Familial, interpersonal, and intrapersonal correlates of drug use: A longitudinal comparison of adolescents in treatment, drug using adolescents not in treatment, and non-drug using adolescents. *International Journal of the Addictions, 23,* 1211-1240.

Nye, F. I. (1958). *Family Relationships and Delinquent Behavior.* New York: Wiley.

Olweus, D. (1993). *Bullying as School: What We Know and What We Can Do.* Cambridge, United Kingdom: Blackwell.

OJJDP (1998). *Serious and Violent Juvenile Offenders.* Washington D.C.: Office of Juvenile Justice and Delinquency Prevention.

Palmer, T. (1991). The effectiveness of intervention: Recent trends and current issues. *Crime & Delinquency, 37*(3), 330-346.

Palmer, T. (1995). Programmatic and nonprogrammatic aspects of successful intervention: New directions for research. *Crime & Delinquency, 41*(1), 100-131.

Park, R. & Burgess, E. (1924). *Introduction to the Science of Sociology.* Chicago: University of Chicago Press.

Patchin, J. W., Huebner, B. M., McCluskey, J. D., Varano, S. P., & Bynum, T. S (2006). Exposure to community violence and childhood delinquency. *Crime & Delinquency, 52*(2), 307-332.

Patternoster, R. & Brame, R. (1998). The structural similarity of processes generating criminal and analogous behaviors. *Criminology, 36*(3), 633-670.

Patterson, G. R. (1980). Children Who Steal. In T. Hirschi and M. Gottfredson (Eds.), *Understanding Crime: Current Theory and Research* (pp. 73-90). Beverley Hills: Sage.

Patterson, G. R. (1982). *Social Learning Approach to Family Intervention.* Eugene, OR: Castilia Publishing Company.

Patterson, G. R., DeBaryshe, B. & Ramsey, E. (1989). A developmental perspective on antisocial behavior. *American Psychologist, 44*, 329-35.

Patterson, G. R., Reid, J. B., & Dishion, T. J. (1992). *Antisocial Boys.* Eugene, OR: Castalia Publishing Company.

Patterson, G. R. & Yoerger, K. (1999). Developmental models for delinquent behavior. In S. Hodgins (Ed.), *Mental Disorder and Crime* (pp. 140-169). Thousand Oaks, CA: Sage.

Pearson, F. S., Lipton, D. S., Cleland, C. M., & Yee, D. S. (2002). The effects of behavioral/cognitive-behavioral programs on recidivism. *Crime & Delinquency, 48*(3), 476-496.

Perkins-Dock, R. E. (2001). Family interventions with incarcerated youth: A review of the literature. *International Journal of Offender Therapy and Comparative Criminology, 45*(5), 606-625.

Polakowski, M. (1994). Linking self- and social control with deviance: Illuminating the structure underlying a general theory of crime and its relation to deviant identity. *Journal of Quantitative Criminology, 10*(1), 41-78.

Pratt, T. C. & Cullen, F. T. (2000). The empirical status of Gottfredson and Hirschi's general theory of crime. *Criminology, 38*(3), 931-964.

Pratt, T. C., Turner, M. G., & Piquero, A. R. (2004). Parental socialization and community context: A longitudinal analysis of the structural sources of low self-control. *Journal of Research in Crime and Delinquency, 41*(3), 219-243.

Quesnel, S., McArdle, P., Brinkley, A., Wiegersma, A., et al (2002). Broken home or drug using peers: "Significant relations"? *Journal of Drug Issues, 32*(2), 467-490.

Rankin, J. H. (1983). The family context of delinquency. *Social Problems, 30*, 466-479.

Rankin, J. H. & Kern, R. (1994). Parental attachments and delinquency. *Criminology, 32*, 495-514.

Raudenbush, S. W. & Bryk, A. S. (2002). *Hierarchical Linear Models: Applications and Data Analysis Methods.* Thousand Oaks, CA: Sage Publications.

Raudenbush, S. W. & Bryk, A. S., Cheong, Y. F., & Congdon, R. T. (2000). *HLM5: Hierarchical Linear and Non-linear Modeling.* Chicago: Scientific Software International.

Rebellon, C. J. (2002). Reconsidering the broken homes/delinquency relationship and exploring its mediating mechanisms. *Criminology, 40*(1), 103-135.

Rebellon, C. J. & Van Grundy, K. (2005). Can control theory explain the link between parental physical abuse and delinquency? A longitudinal analysis. *Journal of Research in Crime and Delinquency, 42*(3), 247-274.

Reiss, A. (1951). Delinquency as the failure of personal and social controls. *American Sociological Review, 16*, 196-207.

Robbins, M. S., Alexander, J. F., & Turner, C. W. (2000). Disrupting defensive family interactions in family therapy with delinquent adolescents. *Journal of Family Psychology, 14*(4), 688.

Rowe, D. & Osgood, D. W. (1984). Heredity and sociological theories of delinquency: A reconsideration. *American Sociological Review, 49*, 526-540.

Salmelainen, P. (1996). Child neglect: Its causes and its role in delinquency. *Crime and Justice Bulletin, 33*, 1-14.

Sampson, R. J. (1985). Neighborhood and crime: The structural determinants of personal victimization. *Journal for Research in Crime and Delinquency, 22*, 7-40.

Sampson, R. J. & Groves W. B. (1989). Community structure and crime: Testing social disorganization theory. *American Journal of Sociology, 94*, 774-802.

Sampson, R. J., & Laub, J. H. (1995). Understanding variability in lives through time: Contributions of life-course criminology. *Studies on Crime and Crime Prevention, 4*(2), 143-158.

Sampson R. J. & Laub, J. H. (1993). *Crime in the Making: Pathways and Turning Points Through Life.* Cambridge, MA: Harvard University Press.

Serketich, W. J. & Dumas, J. E. (1996). The effectiveness of behavioral parent training to modify antisocial behavior in children: A meta-analysis. *Behavior Therapy, 27*, 171-186.

Sexton, T. L. & Alexander, J. F. (2000). Functional family therapy. Juvenile Justice Bulletin. Washington DC: Office of Juvenile Justice and Delinquency Prevention.

Sherman, L. W., Gottfredson, D., MacKenzie, D., Eck, J., Reuter, P., & Bushway, S. (1997). *Preventing Crime: What Works, What Doesn't, and What's Promising?* Washington DC: National Institute of Justice.

Singleton, R. A. & Straits, B. C. (1999). *Approaches to Social Research.* New York: Oxford University Press.

Skinner, B. F. (1953). *Science and Human Behavior.* New York: Macmillan.

Smith, C. A., & Stern, S. B. (1997). Delinquency and antisocial behavior: A review of family processes and intervention research. *The Social Service Review, 71*(3), 382-401.

Snyder, H. N. (2001). Epidemiology of official offending. In R. Loeber & D. P. Farrington (Eds.), *Child Delinquents: Development, Intervention, and Service Needs* (pp. 25-46). Thousand Oaks, CA: Sage.

Snyder, H. N. & Sickmund, M. (2006). *Juvenile Offenders and Victims: 2006 National Report.* Washington, DC: U.S. Department of Justice, Office of Justice Programs, Office of Juvenile Justice and Delinquency Prevention.

Sokol-Katz, J., Dunham, R., & Zimmerman, R. (1997). Family structure versus parental attachment in controlling adolescent deviant behavior: A social control model. *Adolescence, 32*, 199-215.

Sutherland, E. H., Cressey, D. R., & Luckenbill, D. F. (1992). *Principles of Criminology* (11th Ed.). Dix Hills, New York: General Hall.

Steffensmeier, D. J., Allan, E. A., Harer, M. D., & Streifel, C. (1989). Age and the distribution of crime. *American Journal of Sociology, 94*, 803-831.

Tarolla, S. M., Wagner, E. F., Rabinowitz, J., & Tubman, J. G. (2002). Understanding and treating juvenile offenders: A review of current knowledge and future directions. *Aggression and Violent Behavior, 7*: 125-143.

Tate, D. C., Reppucci, N. D., & Mulvey, E. P. (1995). Violent juvenile offenders: Treatment effectiveness and implications for future action. *American Psychologist, 50*(9), 777-781.

Thaxton, S. & Agnew, R. (2004). The nonlinear effects of parental and teacher attachment and delinquency: Disentangling strain from social control explanations. *Justice Quarterly, 21*(4), 763-791.

Thornberry, T. P. (1987). Toward and interactional theory of delinquency. *Criminology, 25*(4), 863-887.

Thornberry, T. P. (Ed.) (2004). *Developmental Theories of Crime and Delinquency: Advances in Criminological Theory (Advances in Criminological Theory)*. New Brunswick, N.J.: Transaction Publishers.

Thornberry, T. P. & Krohn, M. D. (2000). The self-report method for measuring delinquency and crime. In *Measurement and Analysis of Crime and Justice, Criminal Justice 2000* (pp. 33-84). Washington, D.C.: National Institute of Justice.

Thornberry, T. P., Smith, C. A., Rivera, C., Huizinga, D. & Stouthamer-Loeber, M. (1999). *Family Disruption and Delinquency*. Washington D.D.: Office of Juvenile Justice and Delinquency Prevention.

Tienda, M., & Angel, R. (1982). Female headship and extended family composition: Comparisons of Hispanics, Blacks, and non-Hispanic whites. *Social Forces, 61*, 508-531.

Toby, J. (1957). Social disorganization and stakes in conformity: Complementary factors in the predatory behavior of hoodlums. *Journal of Criminal Law, Criminology, and Police Science, 48*: 12-17.

Tolan, P. H. & Gorman-Smith, D. (1998). Development of serious and violent offending careers. In R. Loeber & D. P. Farrington (Eds.),

Serious & Violent Juvenile Offenders: Risk Factors and Successful Interventions (pp. 68-85). Thousand Oaks, CA: Sage.

Tolan, P. H., Guerra, N. G., & Kendall, P. C. (1995). A developmental-ecological perspective on adolescents: Toward a unified risk and intervention framework. *Journal of Consulting and Clinical Psychology, 63*(4), 579-584.

U.S. Census Bureau. (2000). U.S. Decennial Census. Washington, DC: Government Printing Office.

Unnever, J. D., Cullen, F. T., & Agnew, R. (2006). Why is "bad" parenting criminogenic? Implications from rival theories. *Youth Violence and Juvenile Justice, 4*(1), 3-33.

Unnever, J. D., Cullen, F. T., & Pratt, T. C. (2003). Parental management, ADHD, and delinquent involvement: Reassessing Gottfredson and Hirschi's general theory. *Justice Quarterly, 20*(3), 471-500.

Van Voorhis, P., Cullen, F. T., Mathers, R. A., & Garner, C. C. (1988). The impact of family structure and quality on delinquency: A comparative assessment of structural and functional factors. *Criminology, 26*(2), 235-261.

Vazsonyi, A. T. & Flannery, D. J. (1997). Early adolescent delinquent behaviors: Associations with family and school domains. *The Journal of Early Adolescence, 17*(3), 271-293.

Veltman, M. W. & Browne, K. D. (2001). Three decades of child maltreatment research: Implications for the schools years. *Trauma Violence and Abuse: A Review Journal, 2*(3), 215-239.

Wahler, R. G. (1987). Contingency management with oppositional children: Some critical teaching issues for parents. In J. Q. Wilson and G. C. Loury (Eds.), *From Children to Citizens (Vol III): Families, Schools, and Delinquency Prevention* (pp. 112-131). New York: Springer-Verlag.

Wiatrowski, M. D., Griswold, D. B., Roberts, M. K. (1982). Social control and delinquency. *American Sociology Review, 46*, 525-541.

Wallace, J. M. Jr., & Bachman, J. G. (1991). Explaining racial/ethnic differences in adolescent drug use: The impact of background and lifestyle. *Social Problems, 38*, 333-357.

Warr, M. (2002). *Companions in Crime: The Social Aspects of Criminal Conduct.* Cambridge: Cambridge University Press.

Warr, M. (2005). Making delinquent friends: Adult supervision and children's affiliation. *Criminology, 43*(1), 77-105

Wasserman, G. A. & Miller, L. S. (1998). The prevention of serious and violent juvenile offending. In R. Loeber & D. P. Farrington (Eds.), *Serious & Violent Juvenile Offenders: Risk Factors and Successful Interventions* (pp. 197-247). Thousand Oaks: Sage.

Wasserman, G. A., Miller, L. S., & Cothern, L. (2000). *Prevention of serious and violent juvenile offending*. Washington DC: Office of Juvenile Justice and Delinquency Prevention.

Wasserman, G. A. & Seracini, A. M. (2001). Family risk factors and interventions. In Loeber, R. & Farrington, D. P. (eds.). Child Delinquents: Development, Intervention, and Service Needs (pp. 165-190). Thousand Oaks, CA: Sage.

Wells, L. E. & Rankin, J. H. (1988). Direct parental controls and delinquency. *Criminology, 26*(2), 263-285.

Wells, L. E. & Rankin, J. H. (1991). Families and delinquency: A meta-analysis of the impact of broken homes. *Social Problems, 28*(1), 71-83.

Westman, J. C. (1996). The rationale and feasibility of licensing parents. *Society, 34*(1), 46-60.

White, J. L, Moffitt, T.E., Earls, F., Robins, L., & Silva, P.A. (1990). How early can we tell? Predictors of childhood conduct disorder and adolescent delinquency. *Criminology, 28*(4), 507-533.

Whitehead, J. T. & Lab, S. P. (1989). A meta-analysis of juvenile correctional treatment. *Journal of Research in Crime and Delinquency, 26*(3), 276-95.

Wiatrowski, M. D., Griswold, D. B., & Roberts, M. K. (1981). Social control theory and delinquency. *American Sociological Review, 46*, 525-541.

Wilson, J. Q. & Herrnstein, R. (1985). *Crime and Human Nature.* New York: Simon and Schuster.

Wright, J. P. & Beaver, K. M. (2005). Do parents matter in creating self-control in their children? A genetically informed test of Gottfredson and Hirschi's theory of low self-control. *Criminology, 43*(4), 1169-1200.

Wolfgang, M. E., Figlio, R. M., & Selling, T. (1972). *Delinquency in a Birth Cohort.* Chicago: University of Chicago Press.

Wright, J. P., Cullen, F. T., & Miller, J. T. (2001). Family social capital and delinquent involvement. *Journal of Criminal Justice, 29*, 1-9.

Index